THE ULTIMATE YOU

THE ULTIMATE YOU

CHANGE YOUR MIND, TRANSFORM YOUR LIFE

ANDY ANDERSON

FOUNDER & CEO, ULTIMATE YOU

DIVERSION
BOOKS

For more information, email info@diversionbooks.com

Diversion Books
A division of Diversion Publishing Corp.
443 Park Avenue South, Suite 1004
New York, NY 10016
www.diversionbooks.com

Book design by Aubrey Khan, Neuwirth & Associates
Cover design by David Reidy

First Diversion Books edition September 2019
Paperback ISBN: 978-1-63576-635-6
eBook ISBN: 978-1-63576-633-2

Printed in the United States of America

1 3 5 7 9 10 8 6 4 2

I dedicate this book to my little brother Jess.

You taught me the greatest lesson.

When the world seems dark, shine your light brighter.
Never doubt you can make your world better.

CONTENTS

WHY DID I WRITE THIS BOOK?

At age fifteen, my world was a mess. Something happened that shattered my life: My dad, whom I loved dearly, suddenly died. During my early days, my father was my hero. Short and stocky with dark hair and fair skin, my dad ran his own business, building cabinets and furniture. He taught me to be strong, helping me to understand how I need to grapple with hard, tough problems. He taught me about leadership, constantly reminding me, "This is what a leader does," and about kindness—my dad was a man who respected all people, even if they thought and acted differently than he did. He would always stop the car if he saw a homeless person, reach into his pocket, and tell me, "Run over and give this to that man," reminding me how important it was to look after people who needed help or who were less fortunate than we were. Simple lessons like this helped me to grow. His logical, practical, and optimistic life lessons played a huge part in shaping the man I am today.

However, the years leading up to his death had been extremely challenging for me, my mother, and my two little brothers. My father always had a positive outlook on life, but during the last few years of his life, something changed. He struggled with alcoholism and painkiller addiction and was causing a lot of anger, tension, and sadness within our family. He was tortured by internal demons that resulted in an attempted suicide. He had lost his way. And after a solid three years of growing hopelessness and despair, on a sad December night right before Christmas, he had a fatal brain hemorrhage.

After my father died, I wasn't just grieving the death of a loved one—I felt abandoned by him, confused and angry that he was not strong enough to pull himself out of his downward spiral. This loss was agonizing and paralyzing. Shock and numbness gave way to devastation, crushing sadness, and anger with every passing day, but I bore it in silence, putting on a tough persona. Now that my dad was no longer with us, I wanted to step up as the leader of the family, but I was very ill prepared to do so. In fact, I was busy fighting my own demons—the pain of uncertainty about what his loss meant for my family and me—and because of this I was making bad decisions on a daily basis. I was drinking too much and getting into fights constantly. My only interest in life was music, and I was always plugged in, trying to block out my family's painful reality. Meanwhile, my health suffered as I put on tons of weight, drank, and smoked.

A year later, at age sixteen, I hit an all-time low. I had gotten to a stage where I hated myself. I knew I had to do something to turn myself around and make life worth living, but my world just felt gloomy. People around me tried to help, but no one could. Only *I* could, I suddenly realized when I had finally had enough of all the anger and pain. I could no longer be the victim of my past or remain fixed with a narrow mindset. What could I do that would turn me around and help me become who I wanted to be? I was determined to find a way.

●   ●   ●

I'm going to be honest: What followed was the scariest time of my life. Change's friends, Resistance and Fear, love to say hello at these turning points. I knew I had to improve my health and start treating myself right. My excess flab was causing me intense self-hate. Low energy was sabotaging my confidence. My fixed mindset said, "If Rome wasn't built in a day, it probably wasn't meant to be."

Still, I was desperate to get out of my rut, so I started looking for ways to get my body in shape. At my high school in the small town of Ballarat in Australia, they had a great rowing culture, so my school rowing program seemed like a good, readily available option for me. The guys on the rowing team looked like beasts, and they also looked like they were having a blast!

When I joined the rowing team, I was excited about the possibility of personal growth but also very nervous that I would fail. I still remember the first training session as if it were yesterday: We took a 4:30 a.m. 6K run around Lake Wendouree. At the end of the first kilometer, my muscles started to get sore and burn, and by the 3K mark, I almost collapsed. My mouth was dry. I couldn't breathe. I thought I was going to spew right there on the track. I fell to the ground.

It was a freezing-cold morning, yet my whole body was on fire and in severe pain. While the others were running with ease, all I could think of was going home and getting in my bed. Collapsed on the ground, I knew then and there that I had to make a decision: Do I give up and run to my comfort zone, or do I step up and embrace the uncomfortable? If I could just drag my body up and keep going—even if it took me the rest of day—at least I would feel that I had made something of this experience.

And that was exactly what I did: I got up, tapped into that aggression that I had been carrying around, channeled it, and made a move. Now, it was *not* graceful by any standards; it was almost the opposite. I was coughing and spitting as I half-jogged, half-walked the last three kilometers, but, in the end, it was most certainly progress, and, to me, finishing that first session was a huge turning point in my life.

I don't think I would be even writing this book if I had not made the decision to keep going that frigid morning. It forced me to push through my pain and my self-limiting beliefs. I had to believe there would be change on the other side if I was consistent with my actions and effort. That year, I finished the season, lost weight, and became passionate about training my body. Over the next few years, I did every sport I could—boxing, kickboxing, football, running, you name it. I gave up my addiction to junk food and started eating more whole foods, veggies, and leaner meats.

Despite my successful turnaround, it was not a simple upward trajectory from there. Even though I was training seven days a week and had lost over twenty pounds (ten kilos), I still had a bit of a tire around my belly. I felt discouraged. What was I doing wrong? Deep down, I knew I was destined for so much more than where I was in that moment, and I channeled that frustration into action.

I needed to find someone who had achieved what I was striving after, so after I left school when I was around eighteen, I found a health and fitness coach. At first I was skeptical, but I had to overcome my doubts and trust the process. I promised myself that this time it would be different, and with that mindset I started to build momentum. I was taking more action, thinking clearly, and acting with more purpose and passion every day. I was reading more, learning more, and showing up for work and social situations more professionally and positively. Slowly but surely, results started to show—my body was becoming lean and mean, my mind clear and focused.

Finally, I was starting to gain control of myself and my life. And this huge change didn't take years. With the right strategy, I did it within a few months. I felt empowered, filled with a new passion and zest for life, and I decided to dedicate my life to health and fitness. I, too, became a coach and spent the next few years obsessed with learning and practicing my craft, and helping clients achieve amazing results. In turn, this new commitment helped me to become happier and a better leader for myself and others. I had found my purpose and was performing better in all areas of my life.

Still, something was missing; my clients' results were mixed. Not everyone was following through. Some clients would get unbelievable results, and others would self-sabotage. This troubled me deeply. I spent a lot of time thinking about what could be going wrong. What was the missing link?

Eventually, it hit me: Coaching people in nutrition and training wasn't enough. People needed coaching in nutrition, training, *and mindset*. This realization was another major turning point for me and my practice. I decided to dedicate myself to learning all I could about human behavior. I thought of my dad, who had so much wasted talent because he had always felt discouraged, dwelling in negativity and victimhood.

Now when I think about it, everything made perfect sense. If I remained glued to the fixed mindset layered with self-doubt, I could never have changed or developed into who I am today. With my shift in thinking, I was more open to new ideas and new emotional states. It's only through this awareness and searching that I could start to identify and improve upon my own strengths and weaknesses.

I used to think our talents and abilities were set in stone. Whether we were smart or not was not really anything we had control over, and if we weren't lucky sometimes failure could not be avoided. But in reality, talent, success, and wisdom are things we *cultivate*. Once I understood that everything is a learned behavior, it changed my life.

Thoughts and emotions are powerful enough to change our lives entirely, and even the smallest decisions can have profound effects. I always tell my friends and family that they need to stay away from the restrictive "fixed" mindset. One bad experience or setback shouldn't make you feel like a loser. More importantly, you should never allow others to decide what you want in life or what your compelling vision for the future is made of.

*   *   *

Just when I thought everything was going smoothly, another tragedy struck: My beautiful little brother Jessie committed suicide. It was sudden, it was scary, and it shook me to the core. I didn't know he was so depressed, and I was left feeling heartbroken that I couldn't save him, that I couldn't be there for him when he needed his big brother the most. He was such a genuine, beautiful soul. There is not a day that goes by that I don't wish I had done or said something different to change the outcome, to make him open up to me and allow me to help him find a solution to his pain.

A few weeks after Jessie passed, I remember thinking to myself: *There has to be a lesson here. This can't be all for nothing. I won't let his death or story be a waste; he deserves so much better than that.* In the end, the tragedy was a reaffirmation of my mission in life: to help people overcome inner battles and improve their lives. And I now knew they needed the elements of movement, proper nutrition, *and mindset* to thrive.

*   *   *

I've come a long way from the overweight, depressed, angry, irresponsible teenager I once was. My life may not have been the smoothest ride, but I never let my past define who I would become. Since giving up drinking, smoking, and drugs, I've been able to transform all areas of my life in extreme ways. I became an entrepreneur, raising over $600,000 in startup capital over the years and launching my dream business, Ultimate You Change Centers. I turned that business into a seven-figure powerhouse within three-and-a-half years with thirteen locations throughout Australia and thousands of clients. Now, I am expanding Ultimate You further and opening locations across Australia—Melbourne, Sydney, Queensland, Perth—and we are also focused on expanding into the United States and the United Kingdom. We are all so excited about this growth, as our mission is to change as many lives as possible.

Over the years, through my Ultimate You change centers, I have helped more than 150,000 people transform their lives, bodies, and behaviors through my coaching methodologies. I've also helped other entrepreneurs raise capital to build their dream six- and seven-figure passion-based businesses. I've traveled the world, competing internationally in fitness physique championships (including a rank of 1st in Chicago), and eventually winning my Pro Athlete Card.

I hope that this book inspires you by showing you that anything can happen, no matter who you are, where you live, and what has happened in your past. Your past does not dictate your future, and only YOU are the master of your destiny. You may already be on your journey to success and personal evolution, or you may be just starting out. My goal is to show you a whole new world and perspective to explore. On this adventure I don't want to bombard you with complicated tricks or confusing theories. On the contrary, my solutions are simple, straightforward, and organized around a key tenet of success: *no change without challenge.*

So get on board and take the journey with me to a new, passionate you—one who's excited about getting out of bed in the morning and lives a vibrant life, full of purpose. You have nothing to lose but negativity, despair, and hopeless thoughts.

Are you ready for this ride? Let's get started!

YOU ARE WHAT YOU THINK

*"A man is but the product of his thoughts.
What he thinks, he becomes."* —**MAHATMA GANDHI**

The journey to creating epic change and becoming "the ultimate you" is not an afternoon stroll in the park. Actually, it's more like a bloody war with many wins and losses. There will be two steps forward and five steps back at times, but those who achieve this beautiful objective are the ones who choose to fight every single day, especially on the hard days. You know those days: the ones where you want to give up, cry, run away, down a bottle of wine, or eat ice cream instead of stepping up and facing the pressure. Those are the days that heroes are made of, the days that teach us the true lessons of greatness, resilience, courage, and strength. Over the years I have learned that pressure is privilege, hardship is privilege, challenge is privilege, and I have also learned only the ones who recognize this will achieve their full potential.

I designed the Ultimate You program for people who were sick and tired of living life on that up-and-down rollercoaster of weight loss and health. This step-by-step guide has all the tools, techniques, and strategies you need to create the life of your dreams. Within a short time after following this program, you will:

- Find your passion in life and have the drive and direction to reach your goals.
- Be more secure and fired up to take the steps needed to change.
- Be sure of your standards and values and be determined not to violate either.
- Feel unafraid to face your fears and break out of your comfort zone.
- Dare to shoot for the stars...and so much more.

Is it easy? No. And it would be unfair of me to promise you that it is. It's a challenge, and it's going to challenge you mentally, emotionally, and physically, but I know you know that anything worth acquiring is going to be challenging, and in the end it will be so worth it.

WHO WILL BENEFIT FROM THIS BOOK?

- People who are sick of their careers and are searching for one with more passion and purpose.
- People who know they have something special in them and want to achieve their fullest potential.
- People who want to improve their health, relationships, business, or career but need direction to know what steps to take.
- People who wish to move past the self-doubt, fears, and uncertainty to healthier relationships, living situations, and job opportunities.
- People who are ready to take responsibility for their lives.
- People who are in a good place but want to play an even bigger game, achieve more goals, and spend their time in a state of "flow" (see page 17) rather than resistance.

THE FOUR BASIC STAGES OF PERSONAL TRANSFORMATION

Don't think, even for a second, that you do not have the personal power to control your life. You do. Newspapers and history books are full of people who, at one time or another, felt useless and went on to accomplish great feats. It happens every day. Perhaps you know someone who quit his or her unfulfilling office job and has since created an impressive business of their own. Yes, there will be times when unexpected events catch you off guard and overwhelm you, and there will always be a certain number of things you cannot control in life, but the key is realizing that, whatever happens, *you* are in the driver's seat when it comes to your *own* reactions and next steps.

Of course, going through any kind of change is difficult, especially if you don't have any idea where to start. Many of you will likely transcend through four basic stages on this journey:

- **Stage 1: Addict/victim.** You are at the mercy of impulses and addictions, including overeating, drugs, sex, gambling, smoking, shopping—you name it. This place is bad for you and bad for the greater good.
- **Stage 2: Comfort-seeker/follower.** You have begun to break from your addictions and seek comfort in unhealthy ways, such as through junk food or familiar yet unsatisfying workplaces or relationships. Even though you feel comfortable, no meaningful change or development is occurring. As with Stage 1, this place is bad for you and bad for the greater good.
- **Stage 3: Warrior/self-leader.** You begin to feel empowered and take control of your thoughts, emotions, and behaviors. Remember: 90 percent of leadership is self-leadership. At this stage, you are learning to embrace

the uncomfortable, face your inner fears, and challenge yourself mentally and emotionally.

- **Stage 4: Leader.** In the last stage, you have mastered self-leadership and you feel comfortable and confident enough to empower others in amazing ways.

I always tell clients to take charge of the thinking process—the thoughts that bring success and help you maintain it.

I would like to share Stephen's story. Stephen is one of my closest clients, and I really admire the long way he has come. When I met Stephen, it was a chilly Wednesday night, and I had stepped inside the gym to catch up with my workout buddies. Stephen was deep in debt, and creditors were closing in on him. He decided to go for a personal loan to finance his startup, but things didn't go as planned. The bank was demanding payment, and so he sat on the bench holding his head in hands when I first encountered him. I gave him a quick smile and moved past him, but something made me turn around and walk up to him.

"I can see something is troubling you, mate!" I said. "I believe it's best to talk to friends, and maybe I am able to help you." He hesitated for a few seconds but ended up telling me his story, how he had maxed out his credit cards and how his startup had come crashing down. His dreams were shattered. Reflecting on my own struggles, I felt an instant deep connection.

"Failure should never stop work in progress," I said. "That's the only way you can win for a long period of time." With this in mind, I made sure to teach Stephen how to manage his emotions, including negative emotions. I knew it wouldn't be easy for him, especially because his finances weren't in the best shape, but I didn't give up.

"You need to look for your talent to carry you through, mate! You cannot give up without trying. It's time to take charge." Stephen claimed he had lost all his talent, and this really hit me: Stephen's mindset was holding him back.

Since Stephen's startup was a finance consultancy firm, I offered him a job at one of my Ultimate You centers as a finance manager. There, he learned to reshape his thinking, reframe his situation, and take back his personal power so he could move from a victim mentality into a leadership mindset. Exactly one year ago, he was able to relaunch his consultancy firm, which is doing great today.

I must say I'm so glad I caught Stephen at that crucial moment in his life. He was experiencing serious self-doubt: he didn't trust his skills, and, more importantly, he believed that he could never succeed. But he was willing to try a new experience and trusted me enough to be open to my advice and the lessons I wanted to help him learn. The day Stephen decided to change his negative thinking, his life improved and he saw great results. It was his need to get out of pain and into pleasure that motivated him to take action so he could finally transform his situation—and life!

THE THREE-PHASE CHANGE MODEL

To help you along on your own personal transformation journey, I have created a three-phase change model, which will let you know what to expect along each stage. This knowledge will make the process less scary and give you the confidence to push through the pain and transcend doubt and uncertainty.

The first phase of change is **Intellectual**, which can be broken down into three subphases:

1. **Denial:** At first, people tend to deny that anything is wrong with their lives. They might say, "I'm basically a happy person. I'm just under stress." I totally get it. We hate to accept the fact that we need to change because change is difficult, and rationalizing our behavior feels safer than the humiliation and discomfort we must open

ourselves up to when we undertake a meaningful transformation. It's a natural reaction: No one wants to feel
like a loser.

2. **Interested:** When we have played that game of denial
for too long and can't stand the pain of stagnation, we
are forced to confront our situation. This is the point at
which we become "interested in change." And while this
is a great stepping stone, don't cue the confetti just yet.
There are still plenty of opportunities for self-sabotage at
this phase. When it's convenient and when the weather
is good, you make great strides toward change, but when
things get challenging, or when they become inconvenient and things just don't go your way, you step right back
into your comfort zone and associated patterns, habits,
and rituals. At this point, you keep getting the same old,
boring results and continue to hit the same barriers to
your ultimate goal.

3. **Committed:** I love to share this quote with my clients:
"When the pain of staying the same is greater than the
pain of change, then change must happen." This phase
is where it happens. I see people transcend the level of
interested and progress to the level of committed—a
level in which you can sustain long-term change. Once
you feel committed, you will make strides not only when
things are easy, convenient, and the weather is good but
also when things are tough, inconvenient, and it's rain-
ing outside. You will dig deep and embrace the uncomfortable, and little can stop you from charging full speed
ahead.

The second phase of the change model is **Emotional**. We often
underestimate the power of our emotions and the extent to which

they can rule our lives. In truth, most people spend their lives on a reactive rollercoaster, bouncing from one unresourceful feeling to the next and letting them dictate their actions in life. To master this phase, we need to move through the three levels of emotional change, starting with the killer of hopes and dreams:

1. **Resistance:** Resistance is a tool of the ego. Basically, it's a trap to hold you back, to keep you from taking action, and to test the worthiness of your goals. "Resistance is a test," I often tell my clients. It always pops up just before you are about to achieve something amazing, and if you can move forward and take action in the face of it, you will pass the test, and success will be your reward. If you choose to cower from it, however, you fail the test. Until you label Resistance and get good at seeing its many forms, you will always be a victim to the mind tricks it plays on you.

I remember when I truly got to know Resistance, when I shook his hand and told him I would never believe his lies. I had just turned twenty-five and was raising capital for my company Ultimate You. It was my dream and my passion to build a company that would positively change millions of lives, and while I had a business plan, big vision, and relentless drive, I had neither money nor real business experience.

To find the money to start my company, I had to pitch more than 123 people (yes, I still remember the count) and got rejection after rejection. People said my idea wouldn't work, I wasn't good enough, or I was too young. You can imagine the self-doubt and the fear of failure that continued to rise inside me.

Fortunately, as the saying goes, the teacher will appear when the student is ready or when the student most needs it. And it did. When I got to my lowest point and thought the whole plan was going under, I read this brilliant quote from author Steven Pressfield:

Like a magnetized needle floating on a surface of oil, Resistance will unfailingly point to true North—meaning that calling or action it most wants to stop us from doing. We can use it as a compass. We can navigate by Resistance, letting it guide us to that calling or action that we must follow before all others.[1]

After I read that, I was filled with strength and clarity. I said to myself, "It's testing me, and I'm not going to fail." I made a decision then and there to get to know Resistance like a lover and to beat it at its own game. And to do that I needed to transcend to the next level of emotional change:

2. **Acceptance:** At this level, you will start to accept that Resistance, negative emotions, fears, and everything in between are not "wrong" or the "enemy" but rather signals meant to teach us lessons and show us the way. When you embrace this mindset, you can see past the red light to a green light that is beckoning you to charge full speed ahead.

To understand this mindset, try this thought exercise: Imagine you have a piece of paper in front of you. On that piece of paper, you print out all your thoughts and emotions, including all your fears and self-doubt. Now imagine a window out to the world that contains all the things you love, all the challenges, and all the things you value—the good stuff and bad stuff.

Now imagine bringing that paper up to your face. All you can see are your negative thoughts, emotions, and fears. You think that's all there is because, in that moment, you are fused to them and perceive them as part of you. Until you remove the sheet from your gaze, you can't think of solutions or find better things to focus on—you can't see out that window. Once you do, the overwhelming feelings and thoughts get weaker and start to fall away because there is now space to see things as they really are (and not what Resistance wants you to see).

Here's one more exercise: Try closing your eyes and watching your thoughts and emotions from a bird's-eye view. You are now tapping into the observing mind. When you separate yourself from thoughts and feelings, their hold on you releases, and you can choose to focus on more productive things.

3. **Self-love:** Knowing that you can detach from any thought or emotion you want and accept them for what they are frees you to move to the next level: love. This phase is perfectly summed up in this wonderful quote by Robin Sharma: "Change is hard at first, messy in the middle, and gorgeous at the end." When you can really love yourself—your strengths and your weaknesses—and when you can stop comparing the worst parts of yourself to the best parts of others, you will then have the confidence to achieve and sustain true change with your body, business, relationships, career, and well-being.

The final phase of change is **Physical** and begins with the first of three subphases:

1. **Pain:** At the beginning, you will feel the mental and physical pain. To help me deal with the initial agony of challenging myself in new ways, I often remind myself that pain is temporary, but legacy is forever. At this subphase, progress depends on consistency. There is no way of getting around it: If you stop and try again later, the pain will still be there. The only way is to push on. When it feels like it is all too much to bear, say to yourself, "This too shall pass."

2. **Discomfort:** Congratulate yourself when you get to this stage. Remind yourself that everything that was challenging initially becomes easy with consistent effort.

3. **Ease/Adaptation:** Once you have moved past discomfort, you reach the level of adaptation. You have now created a new comfort zone for yourself. Whether this is a physical, mental, or behavioral change, you have become stronger than ever. This is a beautiful place in which to be.

Once you have transcended all three phases of change, you will arrive at the Ultimate version of you! How exciting is that?

Use this model to guide you and to discover where you currently reside in your journey toward greatness. Seeing the road ahead of you gives you certainty, and with certainty comes confidence and strength.

PART 1

FIND YOUR PURPOSE

CHAPTER 1

STRONG VALUES GENERATE POWER

"Try not to become a man of success, but rather try to become a man of value." —**ALBERT EINSTEIN**

Every long journey begins with a first step. In order to outline your vision and goals and become your Ultimate You, you must first assess your core values—who you are and what you want.

While revising my business mission statement before my latest franchise launch, I discovered that the vision I have for my work is really closely tied to what my personal values are—Health and Fitness, Passion, Contribution, Success, Learning and Growth. As entrepreneurs, we spend a lot of time reading and understanding business vision statements, but we rarely think about who we are and what we really want for ourselves.

Our values provide guidance, direction, meaning, and purpose in life. They are our highest priorities—things that are not only important to us but crucial to the way we live life, work, and play. Our values are things that catch our attention and make us passionate. They are the measures we use to figure out whether or not life is turning out the way we want it to, acting as a compass to help us stay on the right track. In my experience, if your actions match your personal values, life is awesome—you feel satisfied and content.

On the other hand, when you start doing things that don't match your values or align with the things you feel are important in life, that's when things start getting worse. You will feel sad and frustrated deep inside, and those negative feelings can start affecting all areas of your life—and what's worse is you might not even realize why you're feeling this way! When you are not clear on what your values are, you don't know what you stand for, and, as they say, "If you stand for nothing, you fall for everything."

It is quite possible that the reason you might have gone through tough times in life is because the way you were living was out of alignment with your core values. As a result, you faced more obstacles than usual, and your life felt like it wasn't going to plan.

Sadly, we are not taught about values at school or at work. Without sounding dramatic, we are almost brought up to become robots—our minds are programmed to execute instructions or some kind of standard operation procedure—or someone else's agenda (parent's, teacher's employer's, etc.). And if you dare to ask any question, or do something differently, you may become an outsider and looked down upon. This is one of the main reasons so many people end up in careers they hate or relationships that don't bring passion. Because they haven't found what they value, what they want, or what they stand for, they conform to a journey of living someone else's truth, not their own.

Don't get me wrong: we most definitely can share the same values as our parents or others, but if you are feeling "stuck" in an area of life, I challenge you to ask yourself: *Am I living via my highest values or someone else's?* You might be surprised by the answer.

WHAT YOU NEED TO KNOW ABOUT VALUES

- **Values are developed over time.** It can take months or years to discover the things that are important to us. Values are born of experience—and thought.
- **Values can vary from person to person.** While one person may have STABILITY as a core value, another might value FREEDOM over anything. Because everyone is unique, there is no one-size-fits-all formula to define one's values.
- **Values change as we transition through different life stages.** This is the biggest reason why you should continuously make it a point to revisit personal values so that you don't feel unbalanced at any point of your life. For example, when you are in college, you might value soaking up technical knowledge more than anything else. The day you complete your studies, financial security and achieving success professionally may become your values. Down the road, when you decide to start a relationship, your values may change again to focus on love and providing a sense of security to your partner. Then when people start a family, they value building a secure future for their kids. After retirement, your highest priority task may be to take a trip around the world and enjoy adventures like never before.
- **Unforeseen life events can affect our values.** My personal experiences have taught me that unexpected life events can have a drastic impact on values. For example, a car accident can change the way you think about financial security and your life. Similarly, experiencing death of a loved one will also force you to

(continues)

rethink your values and priorities, altering your decisions and actions.

- **It's never too late to determine your values.** It's perfectly fine if you haven't thought about connecting with your values—most people even in their twenties, thirties, and forties don't really know who they are or what they stand for. Now's as good a time as any to find out!

DEFINING YOUR VALUES

The first step in finding your purpose is to define your values. Whether you recognize them or not, values exist everywhere around us, and you need to acknowledge them every time you make plans and decisions.

For example, let's say you value your time spent with family. You are presented with an excellent job opportunity, but you are required to work for more than seventy hours every week. No matter how much money you are offered, you will feel internally stressed, and even if you accept the position, you are likely to be unsatisfied with the job. Why? Because aspects of this opportunity conflict with your values. When you know what things matter the most for you in life, you can use them to make more informed decisions about how to live an extraordinary life.

We need to identify the things that have made you feel really good—the times, professionally and personally, when you have been really confident, happy, and were making excellent life choices. In order to discover what your values are, you'll need to examine some key areas of your life, which will give you a realistic picture of what your values are based on the way you live. The following exercise will help you determine your values.

- **Time:** List five activities you spend most of your time on. This is important because people spend their time on activities that they actually *like*, such as sports, skiing, or hobbies, including chess or knitting. You might take out time from your busy schedule to indulge in a hobby you like. If you cannot, you might constantly complain about not having time to go skiing, for example, or whatever it is that you like doing.
- **Energy:** List five activities in which you expend most of your energy and also activities that energize you. It is natural to feel a surge of energy and adrenaline when you are doing something you like. On the other hand, when you are doing something that doesn't interest you, you might feel your energy declining to a point where you don't have any fuel in the tank.
- **Money:** List five ways in which you spend your money. After time and energy, money is the most important resource available to you. Your values will determine, to a large extent, how you spend your money—somehow we tend to go out of the way to come up with money to pay for the things we like. Some people value immediate fulfillment and are more likely to spend on tangibles and consumables—shoes, clothing, food. On the other hand, some people value security and are likely to save or invest.
- **Organization:** Mention five areas where you value organization (perhaps in your office or your garage). Being organized is important for achieving success in life. However, you are more likely to organize and maintain order when it is something you like doing.

Some other questions to consider:

- What career would I work in for free?
- What are the top three to five things I think about most?
- What are the top three to five things I talk about most?

Look at your answers. Are you starting to see a pattern? Think about why these things make you feel this way. Are there any contributing factors that have enhanced your feelings of happiness and pride? Have other people helped you achieve success? Have you experienced feelings of contribution, significance, belonging, or something else?

Now I want you to write down the three answers that came up for you the most during this exercise, from most to least. For example, if "health and fitness" came up the most for you, this is your #1 Value. The second most repeated answer is your #2 Value, and so on.

On pages 9–10 you'll find a list of common core values. Feel free to circle those values that resonate most with you as you complete this exercise. Here are some additional tips for determining your core values:

- **Write whatever comes to your mind without judging yourself or feeling guilty.** Remember you don't have to sound politically correct. Every person is different, and the last thing you should do is allow society or peer pressure to accumulate in your mind and tarnish the thinking process.
- **Don't overthink.** There's absolutely no need to filter your thoughts at this stage. If you keep rethinking and filtering your thoughts, you can't find the right answer.
- **Know that it's OK to go blank at times.** If you cannot come up with a definite answer, come back to it later.

- **Remember that it's perfectly fine if doubts and fear pop up as you perform the exercise.** If they emerge again and again, write them down and figure out how you can overcome them.

Once you've finished this exercise, you should be able to see clearly what your top three values are, and with this vital information you can now start to make decisions around how you want to live your life enjoying, developing, and owning these values.

That's it! If you were expecting some lengthy or complicated stuff, relax! There's nothing fancy or gimmicky about this exercise. This is really a short "values hack" to give you some perspective on what you value most. Once you get familiar with the different kinds of values and how they affect us, mentally and emotionally, you will be in a position of transforming your life for the better. Now you must have the courage to take action!

SOME COMMON CORE VALUES

Accountability	Commitment	Discipline
Accuracy	Compassion	Diversity
Achievement	Competitiveness	Discretion
Ambition	Consistency	Empathy
Balance	Contentment	Elegance
Belonging	Continuous	Efficiency
Being the best	Cooperation	Excellence
Boldness	Creativity	Expertise
Calmness	Courtesy	Fairness
Challenge	Decisiveness	Faith
Cheerfulness	Determination	Fitness
Clear-mindedness	Diligence	Fluency

(continues)

Freedom	Joy	Structure
Fun	Justice	Success
Generosity	Leadership	Support
Grace	Legacy	Teamwork
Hard Work	Love	Thoughtfulness
Health and fitness	Loyalty	Tolerance
Honesty	Obedience	Unity
Independence	Order	Usefulness
Inner Harmony	Security	Vision
Intelligence	Strength	

LIVING YOUR VALUES

Now you should be clear on what your values are and what you want your epic life to be made up of. From here, if you want your life to improve and truly be amazing, you have to dedicate yourself to living these values daily. Nonnegotiable. You must have these values flow through everything that you do—from your career, to your relationships, to your adventures and investments!

For me, this values exercise was a game changer. I started out as a carpenter, which is a great job, but I was not able to truly live my truth via living my core values in that career. Internally, I knew this. I knew that there was something missing, something calling me to WAKE UP and take action, even though at the time it was scary as hell!

Creating the Ultimate You Change Centers was the best way to live my highest values. The business feeds my soul like nothing has ever before. Every day, I live my values of Health and Fitness, Passion, Contribution, Success, Learning and Growth, and all my staff and franchisees get to live these types of incredible values daily too. Nothing is more rewarding than that.

So some personal advice from me: JUST DO IT. Find your passion and values, fight for them, and make them happen. On the other side of that is the Ultimate Life you have been dreaming about.

SUMMING UP

* You are what you value: In order to achieve your goals, you have to figure out what makes you *you*.
* To determine your top values, think about where you spend your time, your energy, and your money and make lists of the top three to five things.
* Narrow down your list of values to three, based on how frequently they appear in your various lists, and be careful not to overthink.
* Success is putting your values into action. Dedicate yourself to living your values daily.

CHAPTER 2

CREATING YOUR VISION

"One day your life will flash before your eyes.
Make sure it's worth watching." —**UNKNOWN**

In 2012, I proudly announced to myself that I would be a world-class entrepreneur and coach. My life at the time was probably giving me a middle finger—"Nice thinking, son!"—but for the next few years I dedicated everything to this mission. This purpose gave a direction to my life. It changed the way I looked at things, how I connected with people, and even what I did with my money. After almost seven years of hard work, my dreams are a reality. I wake up with passion every day and simply love my business, career, and mission in life.

Chances are that you have no clue what you want to do or how you should move ahead with your life—I have seen people who have changed their career aspirations more often than they changed their clothes! I receive dozens of emails from clients or people who follow me online—people in their thirties, forties and fifties who still have absolutely no idea about what they want to do with themselves.

First of all, there's nothing to worry about because this is a struggle almost every person goes through at some point. Rather than stress about it, let's look at this with a solution-focused mindset and create some change, shall we? At whatever point you are, this is the right time for you to clearly define what you want to do with your life.

Now, enough talk. Let's dig into some action!

STRATEGIES FOR CREATING A COMPELLING VISION

So many people don't even realize that they are sent to Earth for some higher purpose and that it's their job to figure out what that is. There's no reason for you to be comfortably resting on your couch, eating nachos, and passively contemplating the purpose of your life. Rather, you should be working your ass off to *actively* discover what's important to you. Here are some strategies to help you do just that:

Lesson 1: Explore Your Passions

In August 2011, Gerlinde Kaltenbrunner scaled K2 (Mount Godwin-Austen), the second highest mountain in the world. This gave her the distinction of becoming the first woman in history to summit all fourteen of the world's 8,000-plus-meter peaks without supplemental oxygen. *National Geographic* asked the forty-two-year-old Austrian why she climbs. She said she feels completely herself when in the mountains with only the bare essentials. "Nothing else exists, only the climb."

She wasn't always so bold. As a teenager, she dreamed of becoming a professional mountaineer but didn't know how, so she became a nurse. Finally, in 2003, she courageously devoted herself only to climbing. "The most important thing," she told *National Geographic*, "is to have this passion inside. It's not about what other people say is best for you—listen to your soul, your body, your gut instincts. If you really love something, you'll find a way to reach it. But without passion, it's pointless."

If you knew you could not fail, what would you do? Who would you be? Perhaps you would like to get a bestselling novel published, or create new computer software, or make a killing in the stock market, work for a company that inspires you to be better every day, or even own an Ultimate You Change Center. Perhaps you too would desire to scale a mountain like Gerlinde Kaltenbrunner or work to conserve wildlife like Steve Irwin did. When you find your purpose, you feel "in flow," you get lost in what you do, and there is this amazing internal energy that drives you forward no matter what the obstacle is. This puts you in touch with your essence. You get fired up, and there's no stopping you.

To set up the right mental landscape to discover your vision, I always suggest starting with asking yourself the following questions:

- If there was nothing holding me back, what would I create or have?
- What does my ideal or my ultimate career look like?
- What do I dream/fantasize about?
- What do I love to read about?
- What gives me energy?
- What would I regret not having tried?
- What sparks my creative juice?
- What would I do for free?

Keep in mind that you cannot set limits on yourself during this process of inquiry. You need to free your mind and be open to all the positive possibilities of life. It's the only way to tap into what will truly fulfill you. I spent years searching for my truth, and after asking question after question, the answer that kept coming up for me was "Ultimate You Change Centers." I remember finally accepting that I needed to make that vision a must!

Do you feel any closer to knowing your personal vision? I bet you do. If not, don't fret. You'll get there. Creating your vision is an ever-evolving thing, something that you create and then improve day by day and tweak it to make it a reality. Do the work—it's the only way.

Lesson 2: Explore What Would Make You Feel Like a Leader

Everyone wants to feel like they are successful and fully in control of their lives, and everyone wants to have some kind of impact on the world around them. And we each have a different definition of what would make us feel this way. To discover your definition, here's a short exercise: Make a list five things, in order of priority, that would make you feel like a leader. (You may wish a million dollars—who doesn't want to have more money!—but let's be more practical.)

High on your list might be to become a clinical psychologist and help lessen a person's struggle through life or to become a coach and help people transform their mindset, nutrition, and training. Perhaps it's status and might come from, for instance, being elected to your local city council? Perhaps it's respect that might come from being given a professorship in Oriental languages at the University of Melbourne. Perhaps it's being influential that might come from being the CEO of a big company, working on the reduction of global warming.

Or perhaps the items on your list are not so grandiose. Perhaps it's not winning the Nobel Prize in physics but getting a local award for your invention. Maybe you don't care about making the *New York Times* bestseller list and reaching a wide readership but want to write something that will inspire a specific group of individuals. Maybe you don't want to be an entrepreneur but, instead, want to be a leader in the company you work for and mentor incredible staff members. Figure it out!

Lesson 3: Consider What You Are Good At

When was the last time you asked yourself, "What am I good at?" Ponder this question, and there is a good chance you will discover things about yourself that you hadn't realized.

For instance, my friend's mother loves to write song lyrics and recently had a local guitarist put music to her words. She didn't realize she had this talent until late in life when her grandchild asked her to sing her a song and, spontaneously, lyrics popped out of her head. If this serendipitous event hadn't occurred, she would never have used her natural talents fully.

It's important not to be overly critical of yourself at this stage in the process. Remember that people are smart in different ways. You can be great in math but have two left feet. You may be unable to utter an intelligible sentence but can sing like Celine Dion. Don't focus on what you can't do. Focus on what you're good at and where you have the most potential to succeed if you put all your might into developing those skills.

What might you be good at that you have not tapped into? Most likely, it's something that comes naturally to you. Perhaps it's math, or drawing, or writing, or computers. Make a list of all the things you do well.

Lesson 4: Follow Your Inner Guidance System

> "Don't ask yourself what the world needs. Ask yourself what makes you come alive and then go do that. Because what the world needs is people who have come alive."
> **—HOWARD THURMAN**

If you're unsure about what you want to do in life, listen to your mind and body. Pay attention to how you feel when you are engaged in an activity. Do you feel bored or drained? Do you just want to get out of there? Trust me when I say that your gut feeling will not betray you in these instances. If something doesn't feel right and you continue to perform the activity over days, months, or years, the result will be low self-esteem, despondency, or even depression.

On the other hand, when you notice that an activity enlivens and engages you every time you perform it, that's an excellent sign that you've discovered a true passion. Congratulations! The feeling you get when engaging in a passion is similar to what Russian psychologist Mihaly Csikszentmihalyi describes as a "flow" state:

FINDING YOUR "FLOW"

"Flow" is a description of experiences we have that involve our full attention, engagement, focus, and capacities. During these experiences, things like self-consciousness and anxiety all dissolve. One's perception of time becomes altered, and time tends to quicken, almost like the old saying, "Time flies when you are having fun." The key to achieving flow is to create the following conditions in the tasks you choose:

- There is an intense focus on the task at hand.
- There is a merging of action and awareness.
- There is a sense of control while undergoing the task or activity.
- There is a sense of the experience being rewarding.
- The task produces immediate results and feedback—i.e., small victories.
- The immediate feedback or results make the task a challenge that then involves calibration to improve and advance.

- The challenge should have a balance of difficulty and perceived confidence to attempt the task. If it is too easy or too hard the task becomes disengaging.

If you can achieve flow, you can use it to break away from negative thought patterns and get the brain into the habit of being happy, and we can use this state of being as a method or guide to identify what our passions and values are.

We can—and should—adapt a lifestyle in which we create "flow" experiences on a daily basis. If you can find jobs or work that produces flow, props to you! Flow can be achieved in factory jobs, if you find them engaging, challenging, or slightly fun. It can even be achieved while solving math equations or playing Frisbee or video games. Try to think about where you have achieved flow in your own life. Some people find that daily exercise or workouts are the cure for their own depressions and anxieties. Figure out what works for you!

Lesson 5: Create Your Life Purpose Statement

Did you ever envision your mission in life? The one thing that would make you feel that your time on this Earth made a positive difference? Most of us have at one time or another. US President John F. Kennedy wanted to put a man on the moon by the end of the 1960s. Albert Einstein wanted to solve the mystery of space and time. Thomas Edison wished to create an invention that people needed.

What were you born to do? Here are some ideas:

- Help people learn how to conserve energy to help save the planet.

- Make a million dollars so you can help support your parents in their old age.
- Coach people to transform their lives and bodies.
- Invest as much money as you can in your children's education so they can have a better life than you did.
- Teach underprivileged children to learn to read so they can have more success in life.
- Become a successful entrepreneur and make enough money to help support cancer research.

I found my purpose in life when I decided to burst my small "personal comfort" bubble—the bubble that's deeply connected to our thoughts and fits nicely inside our comfort zone. Trust me when I say that the day you decide to step out of this bubble, you will be able to see things more clearly, with perspective and with a wider view that includes others. You will begin to see the needs of others and feel their suffering, and you will be moved to help make their lives better and lessen their suffering. As we go about our daily work, tying our actions to a greater purpose makes us true leaders.

"The two most important days of a man's life are the day on which he was born and the day on which he discovers why."
—ERNEST T. CAMPBELL

In this path, it doesn't matter what specific actions you take or skills you learn to make people's lives better. What career you choose is not important—you can always change your career and learn new skills later. What matters is your vision of the Ultimate You—the you that will leave a lasting mark on those around you and the world. Once you can define that epic, transcendent version of yourself that you aspire to, you'll be well on your way to living a life of passion and purpose.

THE SUCCESS BOARD

In Chapter 1, you determined your top core values in life, and in this chapter I challenged you to explore your passions, consider your strengths, and determine your purpose statement. Now we will use everything we have learned thus far to create your life's vision. To begin, try this exercise:

1. **Take out a piece of paper or create an online document and write out your story, as it is now, in all areas of your life:**
   - Body image
   - Relationships
   - Health
   - Work
   - Career
   - Community
   - Finances

2. **Write out your story as you would like it to be.** Feel free to add more details to make your story as realistic as possible. Think of your life as a work in progress. (At the end of this book, you will again write out your story—be prepared to be astonished at all the changes!)

3. **Create a "success board" that visually defines this epic future.** Basically, this is a poster board in which you create a collage of images that you've cut out from various magazines, online photos, and other media sources. It's a visual tool to help you define who you want to become—the car you wish to drive, the house you wish to live, and the city, the career to which you aspire, the body you want to have (be realistic), the places you'd like to visit, and so on. For

your success board to really work for you, focus not just on what you want but also on how you feel. For instance, if you love the sensations of skiing downhill, don't just have a photo of your log cabin on the ski slope; include a photo of a skier flying down the mountain. When you place a vision board where you see it often, you focus on it and unknowingly end up doing short visualization exercises throughout the day. (For more on visualization, see Chapter 6.)

YOUR PERSONAL CODE OF HONOR

Once you've created the vision of what you want your life to be, it's time to set a personal code of honor, which is a dividing line that mentally and emotionally sets you apart from other people. This code also makes you accountable—it keeps you focused on who you want and need to be on a day-to-day basis. It will allow you to live your truth. A personal code is also a physical, emotional, and mental limit we establish to protect ourselves from being manipulated, used, or violated. Successful people take responsibility for their actions, and they continually remind themselves of what needs to be done—and avoided—in order to move closer to their goals.

Our code of honor has two main functions:

1. **It helps us to define who we are and what we aspire to in all situations in terms of emotions, thoughts, and behaviors.** It also helps us to establish what we want and what we stand for, as well as what our rights are as powerful and passionate human beings.

2. **It helps us establish what we do NOT want and will NOT accept in our lives.** It tells us which behaviors we find ob-

jectionable and when other people are acting in ways that are not OK. It lets us know when to say NO, when it's our right to defend ourselves, when to call out or eliminate negativity or naysayers from our lives. It also gives us permission to have differences of opinion when dealing with others.

A powerful code begins with the recognition that we have not only the right but also the duty to take responsibility for how we allow others to treat us. This is a huge part of you beating or avoiding the dreaded "people pleaser syndrome!" Here are some additional tips for creating your personal code:

- Start each sentence with, "It is my right and responsibility to…," or "I always…"
- Make sure each element of the code emotionally resonates with you.
- Make sure each element solves a problem, keeps you focused, or protects you in some way.
- Make sure each element reflects your personal code of conduct and how you choose to live your life.

I want to help you create and set a clear and powerful code of honor, so here is a list of possible elements to get you started:

- It's my right NOT to feel guilty when I say no to someone.
- It's my right and responsibility to be happy, passionate, and fulfilled.
- It's my right to call out anyone who mistreats me.
- It's my right to question people's opinions or beliefs.
- It's my right to keep calm under pressure.
- It's my right to do what I say and my responsibility to be a person of integrity.

- It's my responsibility to create an environment that is aligned with my values and aids me in success.
- It's my responsibility to do more with less.
- It's my right and responsibility to remove negative people from my life.
- It's my right and responsibility to defend myself from an attack of any kind.

OK, now it's your turn. Start by listing twelve to fifteen sentences as part of your personal code of honor that will help you define how you live an extraordinary life. Once you have your success board and your personal code of honor established, nothing can stop you from making your dreams a reality. Think of your life as a book that is being written. Rewrite your story and become the person—and the leader—you were meant to be.

Create your vision. Find your purpose. Live your passion. And do it with honor.

SUMMING UP

- Explore your values, strengths, and passions to create your life's vision.
- Imagine your life as your "story." Are you writing the story you want to live? By writing it, you set the stage to begin living it.
- Creating a life purpose statement and a success board will help you to clarify and visualize the life you want to live.
- A personal code of honor will make you accountable for your thoughts and actions, empower you to remove negative influences from your life, and enable you to live your best life.

CHAPTER 3

SETTING THE RIGHT GOALS

"If you want to be happy, set a goal that commands your thoughts, liberates your energy, and inspires your hopes." —**ANDREW CARNEGIE**

By this time, you likely know your vision in life. Great! You are a warrior charged to march down the road to strong leadership. Now you need to set goals to achieve that vision.

The goals we set for ourselves are tied to our dreams, desires, and things we want to achieve in life. When you have clear goals, you progress towards them more rapidly, and this makes you happier, feeling more fulfilled and satisfied with life.

All leaders set goals, as goal setting enables you to take control of your life's direction. And it serves as a benchmark to determine success. You may wish to start a business in organic farming, but simply wanting it won't make it happen. You need well-defined steps: How much land do you need? How much will it cost to buy? How much startup capital is required? How much backup money must you have if you don't make any profit the first two years? And so on.

As you can see, a bit of work is involved in setting your goals and ascertaining the steps needed to accomplish them. If you don't take the time to systematically figure these things out, you won't have a clear direction, may continue to flounder, and won't become the leader that you know you have in you.

Let's get started!

STRATEGY 1:
SET YOUR "CHANGE" GOALS

Every goal you set should have the following six characteristics:

Challenging (Yet Achievable)

You want to set goals that require you to "raise the bar" and bring the greatest personal satisfaction. These are goals that push you out of your comfort zone but not so far that you land in quicksand. If your goals are too easy, then they are merely tasks, just things on your to-do lists. They need to challenge you, engage you, and force you to focus and rise up to the occasion. Challenging goals will help you grow.

Heartfelt

You must be emotionally connected to your goals—they should fire you up, be important to you, and have value. If it feels meaningful, you are more likely to try harder and persevere when things get hard or don't go your way.

*　　*　　*

Actionable (With a Deadline)

Set goals in which you can plan your action steps NOW. It's wonderful that you may wish to become a sculptor someday when you retire, but that may be far in the future. Your task now is to get fired up and get going! Pressure creates diamonds. You need to put pressure on yourself to be chipping away at the tasks that need to get done daily in order to get to where you want to be. Your level of urgency will directly affect how much you get done and how much action you take. Don't say, "I will lose the weight over a span of fifty years"—cultivating motivation daily over a fifty-year period is incomprehensible. Starting with daily and weekly goals will keep the pressure on you to work.

Nonnegotiable

Your goal must be a given, a must. It has to be achieved—you are not going to dabble or give up in the face of adversity. You are going to be absolutely committed to the process and success. You owe it to yourself to build the life you want and be all you can be.

Geared for the Greater Good

Sometimes being motivated for just our own "personal goals" isn't enough, but when we know that the goal could make the lives of our loved ones, or our community, or even the planet, better, then it becomes easier to maintain momentum and motivation when there are obstacles. Also, setting goals that serve others can make us feel connected and more accomplished. For instance, inventing a plastic bag that can carry twice the weight of those generally used in the supermarkets may make you a million bucks, but it will pollute the environment and encourage people to continue to engage in behaviour that's harmful to the earth and the future of mankind. Create something in your life that will make the world a better place for your children and grandchildren, ensuring their successful survival, and you will work harder to make it happen.

Exact

Write out your goals in detail and be specific—no fluff. Saying that you want to be a millionaire is pie in the sky. You need to state specifically how much you wish to make a month for the next ten years by, for instance, creating a more efficient solar panel. Being vague will not serve you in getting what you want. Vague goals produce vague results.

STRATEGY 2: PRIORITIZE YOUR GOALS

You may have lots of goals—and I hope you do—but you need to figure out which ones have the highest priority. You may have to decide if you wish to pursue a career and then have a family, or have your family first and then devote yourself to a career as your kids get older. Setting your goals according to the high priorities in your life will give your goals an attainable order. Not doing this, in contrast, can result in scattered and sometimes too many goals, leaving you too little time to devote to each one.

•   •   •

STRATEGY 3:
BE A PRAGMATIC OPTIMIST

When setting a goal, keep in mind the Law of Attraction: like energy attracts like energy. That means positivity attracts positivity, and negativity attracts negativity, so think positively and focus on what you will do—not on what you won't do.

STRATEGY 4:
BREAK DOWN GOALS
INTO MANAGEABLE CHUNKS

Here are a few lessons to help you organize goals in different areas of your life, as well as making them specific and achievable:

Lesson 1: Divide Your
Goals into Short- and Long-Term Goals.

For short-term goals, think about what you can manage in the next thirty days. For long-term goals, think about what you want to accomplish over the next year to ten years. For example, losing five pounds is a short-term goal; getting your MBA is a long-term goal.

Lesson 2: Break Down
Your Goals into Relevant Categories.

Set goals to cover all aspects of your life in which you wish to grow and evolve into a leader. To get motivated, jot down five short-term goals and one long-term goal that you want to accomplish for each of the following areas (I've started you off with some examples):

- Nutrition
- Exercise
- Mindset
- Family
- Career
- Spirituality

For example, under "Nutrition," you may want to include the following:

- Short-term goal: Give up all diet sodas by the end of two weeks.
- Short-term goal: Increase my water intake by sixteen ounces each day.
- Long-term goal: Give up all processed food by the end of the year.

When it comes to writing out your goals, here are some additional tips:

1. **Make sure they are framed in a positive way.** Write "will" rather than "would like to" or "might"—for example, "I will spend an hour online tomorrow marketing my art," not "I would like to spend an hour online tomorrow marketing my art." (Say both statements out loud, and you will immediately feel how much more motivating the first statement is.)

2. **Write your goals out in specific detail so you have a road map to follow.** This will help to prevent you from wandering off randomly. You can even create a chart or grid,

and each time you've met goal, put a checkmark in the appropriate box.

GOAL	1	2	3	4	5
Nutrition					
Exercise					
Mindset					
Family					
Career					
Spirituality					

Lesson 3: Start Small.

Accomplishing goals is all about baby steps, not grand leaps. Choose one thing to improve incrementally every day, like replacing apple pie with an apple to meet your goal of eating healthier. Eating fruit, like an apple, a banana, or a cup of berries, is something most people can commit to doing consistently, and succeeding at this small step will give you the confidence and motivation to take a bigger leap, like giving up diet sodas for Kombucha, a fermented drink (more on "Progressive Overload" in Chapter 4).

Lesson 4: Create a Backup Plan.

Sometimes, even with the best planning and action, circumstances may intervene that prevent you from reaching your goals, particularly long-term goals. For instance, you might have been accepted into an MBA program at your local university but just found out your mother has breast cancer, and you must be available for her and can't go. To avoid feeling discouraged and losing hope, have additional paths made for achieving your goals—Plan As, Plan Bs, and even Plan Cs and Ds. This way, if one plan doesn't work out, you can try another angle. You have a backup. In other words, be committed to the goal but flexible in your path to getting there.

Lesson 5: Make Your Goals Visible.

To remind yourself every day of what it is you intend to do, write your goals on index cards and place them in visible places: walls, desk, computer monitor, bathroom mirror, or refrigerator. Each morning when you wake and each night before you go to bed, read your goals aloud and then pause for a second, close your eyes, and visualize them completed.

STRATEGY 5:
PREPARE TO WORK HARD

I know that you are now a charged-up warrior, but becoming a leader won't happen overnight! Rather, small successes build upon one another and create momentum. In other words, goal setting is ongoing, not just a means to an end, so be prepared for a long but satisfying journey toward leadership. Set a long-term plan, monitor your progress, and always be open to revising the plan if you aren't getting the results you want. Bottom line: Persist until you get what you want, and remember that it's a long journey—sometimes smooth, sometimes bumpy, sometimes closed off—but that you have the will, fortitude, and dexterity to push through the obstacles and take the occasional detour when necessary, until you arrive at your final destination.

Our goals come in all shapes and sizes. What was your goal when you woke up this morning? What is your goal when you finish reading this book?

SUMMING UP

- Leaders set goals: Goal setting lets you take control of your life's direction and also provides a benchmark for determining whether or not you are succeeding.
- The right goals are CHANGE: Challenging yet achievable, Heartfelt, Actionable, Nonnegotiable, Geared for the greater good, and Exact.
- Goals should be prioritized and broken down into manageable tasks.
- Goal setting is ongoing: Set both short- and long-term plans, along with backup plans, and then continue to monitor your progress, modifying as needed.

PART 2

CHANGE YOUR MINDSET

CHAPTER 4

STOP DOUBTING YOUR POTENTIAL

"I've had a lot of worries in my life, most of which never happened." —**MARK TWAIN**

H as your day ever started like this?: *What if I screw up this presentation?! What if my boss thinks I'm incompetent? I look terrible today. Blah! I just cannot afford to miss out on this opportunity. The weather is crappy, and so am I!*

Well, hold your thoughts right here. You haven't yet stepped out of your bed, and you are thinking about failing at your presentation and getting stuck in a traffic jam and a million other negative thoughts. Many of you might be laughing at this story, but isn't this something we do every day without noticing?

Lots of my clients keep asking me whether or not negative thinking and self-doubt are two of the biggest problems holding people back from success and happiness. The answer is a big YES! Negative thinking—or self-doubt, as I prefer to call it—is perhaps the biggest obstacle to achieving your full potential. It is a tool your mind uses to depress and suppress you. As you already know, life is full of unexpected events, and if you wake up every day with a series of horrible scenarios playing inside your head, you will stay down in defense mode forever. What's more, negative thinking can even adversely affect your physical health! In fact, a large study conducted at the University of California at San Diego found that the more strongly Chinese-Americans believed that their lives were hexed or ill-fated—based on Chinese superstitions—the earlier they died![1]

We all create a narrative in our minds that describes our story as we live it. This narrative affects how we perceive ourselves and unconsciously guides our actions, decisions, and feelings. Some of us love creating "snowballs"—the negative thoughts that keep getting bigger—and there comes a point when they completely obscure our ability to focus on the situation at hand.

If you have a positive self-image, you feel confident in your ability to get what you want from life and take the actions necessary to make that happen. If you want to lose weight, the voice inside your head might say, "Okay, I want to lose twenty pounds (ten kg). I'm going to hit the gym every night for a forty-five-minute workout and reduce the amount of bad fat and sugar from my diet."

On the other hand, if you have a negative self-image, your script might say, "Why should I even try to work out? I'm fat, I'm ugly, and I'll never lose weight." So you end up doing nothing, which sabotages your goals, because your negative internal monologue has you locked into an unhealthy lifestyle.

> *"I've failed over and over and over again in my life, and that is why I succeed."* —**MICHAEL JORDAN**

OVERCOMING FEAR

If fears stop you from taking the steps needed to get what you want out of life, you are far from alone. Humans are fearful creatures. I'm not talking about fear of snakes or of fire but fear as it relates to mindset—what's inside our heads, our misconceptions or limiting personal beliefs. We may feel afraid of speaking up at work, thinking that we will be judged for our words and thoughts. We may feel afraid to tell our partners that we need them to assume more responsibility with the children. We may feel afraid to take up a particular task, assuming we will fail. We may be afraid of criticism, rejection, and being judged as a person who isn't good enough.

The problem is that such fears can keep us living in a flight/fight response and overwhelm our coping capacities. When we are fearful, we end up doing nothing and staying exactly where we are now. Fear—a necessary survival mechanism that is designed to keep us alert for danger in our quest for survival—can wind up creating dangerous negativity instead: "I can't do that," "I'll never succeed," "I don't have the right stuff to get what I want." The more you fear something, the worse these negative feelings can get.

Of course, it may not be easy to get past your fears. At first, they will be embedded in your mind, like we discussed in the three phases of change, but once you get past the Resistance stage, you can easily overcome them. If you don't face and befriend them now, you will be left stuck in self-doubt and limited beliefs—they will squeeze your dreams out of you like a boa constrictor.

Let's discuss—and diffuse—some of the basic fears that hold us back and suffocate us.

FEAR OF FAILURE

"I have not failed. I've just found 10,000 ways that won't work." —THOMAS EDISON

Do you avoid doing things to avoid failure? Welcome to the crowd. Fear of failure is one the most crippling fears because it rules over our actions and decisions. If we are too afraid to pursue our dreams or try something new because we are convinced we will fail, we don't take the necessary steps to become a warrior/leader.

Fear of failure comes from an unhealthy aversion to risk because you feel vulnerable. What if all your efforts to get into that graduate program, to get the high paying job, to get that fabulous date, to bid on the house of your dreams will come to naught and you lose to yourself? You start thinking about it. Is it even worth trying again?

What counts as failure differs from person to person. To some getting an A- means failure while for others it's getting a C. For some not getting the gold medal at the Olympics means failure; for others it's not hitting the tennis ball back.

Overcoming Fear of Failure:

It is time you begin to accept failure as inevitable and rejection as a fact of life. Yes, you have to understand that life is imperfect, and this is okay. Here are some ways to help you accept this, so you will be free of self-defeating fears and filled with love:

1. **Take risks.** I'm the kind of person who has overcome fear by throwing myself into deep water. I've told myself, "Swim or drown," and, trust me, this brutal approach worked. To do this, you need to change your mindset and see failure as a stepping stone, not an end. When you fail, reassess the situation and ask yourself what could you have done differently or better to achieve a different outcome.

2. **Detach from the outcome.** Once you understand that success rarely comes without some failure along the way and that failure is a part of life and not something that is because of YOU personally, it is so much easier to embrace fear!

3. **Explore new possibilities.** If you feel you've failed at something, ask yourself: What have I learned from this failure?

How can I improve for next time? What will I not do again?

4. **Stop imagining the worst-case scenario.** If you have the habit of considering all that could possibly go wrong, change the way you think now. Instead, work on your problem-solving skills, and figure out how you will handle the situation if something bad happens.

5. **Stand straight.** Yes, you need to stand with your spine erect! When you are afraid, worried, depressed, or sad, you tend to slouch. This drooping posture can make any person feel even worse. In his workshops, motivational speaker Tony Robbins always tells people that you can change the way you feel by changing your physical posture. Stand up tall, pull your shoulders back, stick your chest out, and raise your chin. Such a "confident" stance is associated with power and authority, changing your state from negative to positive.

FEAR OF SUCCESS

Fear of success might sound crazy, but it's a big stumbling block for many. Why would this be? Because having more freedom, having more money, having more recognition, having a bigger promotion can create huge changes in your life, and change is scary. There are gains, but there are also potential losses. Fear of success can bring misguided or imagined potential restrictions, responsibilities, and changes in our lives, such as:

- **Lack of time:** Success will also likely mean more responsibilities and hours worked. This means less time to study, relax, do exercise, or even be with your family and friends. Some people are scared of success because they don't want to miss out on quality sleep!

- **Conflict over money:** More money is great, but it might also mean that you will make more money than your partner does, and this could cause a rift in your marriage. Or it may mean that people will be coming to you for loans, which will cause friction in those relationships.
- **Unpredictable circumstances:** Fear of success falls within the broader category of "fear of change," and change is often associated with the unknown. As the saying goes, the devil you know is better than the one you don't know. Often we feel that it's easier to stay where we are then to be thrust with new and unpredictable circumstances.

Overcoming Fear of Success:

Although it's good to think things through, too much caution is limiting. If you never venture anywhere new, or try anything different, you will stay stuck in the same place. As Albert Einstein once said, "Insanity is doing the same thing over and over again and expecting different results." How can you overcome a fear of success or change?

1. **Recognize it.** Acknowledge that you have this fear. Then you can begin to develop strategies to work around it.

2. **Use models.** Think of successful people who dared to venture out and try something new and how their life changed for the better as a result.

3. **Make a list of what matters. Monitor it.** Write down what changes you want to make in your life, but also write down

what changes you DON'T want to make in your life, the things you want to keep constant. For example, maybe you want to focus on your music but don't want to lose sight of your family. Make sure your goal-setting process incorporates both lists and monitor them regularly.

FEAR OF REJECTION

When we opened our first Ultimate You Change Center, I was not well versed in marketing—plus, we had no money to put into marketing. So what did we do? Cold calling and street sales! I even dressed up in red morph suits and walked around with a clipboard to get attention and sign people up to memberships!

I cannot count the times I was rejected, hung up on, or told to "piss off" when approaching people to tell them about the things I loved most in this world. At the start, I was shocked, hurt, and, to be honest, ANGRY, but at the time I had no option but to persist, to reframe the situation and do everything in my power to learn from it and have fun! It was painful, scary, and, at times, smashed my ego to pieces, but the beautiful thing about this process is that after your ego is smashed to pieces, if you continue to persist, your ego is reborn—stronger, tougher, and more resilient than ever! This helped me become the leader I am today.

No one likes to be rejected. We all need the acceptance and acknowledgement, but we also need to understand that rejection is unavoidable. Even the smartest and most able and beautiful will experience rejection. It's a fact of life. At some time in our life, odds are that we are going to be slighted, turned down for a job, not get into the college of our choice, or, perhaps worst of all, fail in our love life.

This is all normal.

But if you have low self-esteem, you have a desperate need to please people so they will like and accept you. Any rejection can rip you to pieces, and you may unknowingly self-sabotage. You may lash out at others, afraid that rejection is about to slap you in the face. You may reject a loved one, believing he or she is going to reject you first. You may not go to a job interview, convinced the employer will not hire you.

Overcoming Fear of Rejection:

A confident leader accepts rejection as a part of the risk of living and knows that to grow we have to step outside of our comfort zone. A confident leader doesn't take rejection personally but rather views it from a point of curiosity in the other person—rejection is the other's loss, not your own. A leader knows that he or she must face rejection daily in order to condition themselves and build emotional resilience in this space. The more you face it, the easier it gets. To overcome fear of rejection, I use one method regularly: Progressive Overload.

Progressive Overload was originally designed for physical training. Developed by a man named Thomas Delorme, MD, while he was rehabilitating soldiers after World War II, it involves gradually increasing the stress placed on your body during therapy or training in a way that helps you gain muscle size, as well as strength and endurance. How do I adapt this method for combating the fear of rejection?

1. **Start small.** It could be asking for a discount at the store or starting a conversation with a stranger. Start with embracing the uncomfortable, and then ramp it up: Ask for a raise or approach investors to raise capital for your business. You'll see that the more you do it, the stronger you'll get—being able to handle more rejection every time. It's about conditioning your ego every day to handle this type of pressure, and, I'm telling you, if you commit to this type of conditioning, your world will completely transform.

FEAR OF NOT BEING ENOUGH

How many times have you wanted to start your own business but felt you weren't smart enough to succeed? The fear of not being smart enough, good enough, productive enough, talented enough, competent enough, or pretty enough is another reason why we often resist change. Nothing sabotages dreams as powerfully as self-doubt—the feeling that you don't deserve, aren't worthy, or are incapable of achieving what you want in life, that you just don't have the right stuff.

Overcoming the Fear of Not Being Enough:

This one involves a little pushing through to achieve a change in your thinking. Even if you doubt yourself, decide that you WILL achieve your goal, just as I forced myself to get up from the ground and finish my run when I was half dead so I could be on the rowing team. If I gave in to my self-doubt, you wouldn't be reading this book now. It was only because I was furious at myself for being so negative, for being such a loser, for wanting to give up, that I managed to crawl up and eventually make it to the finish line. Some other tips:

- **Tell yourself that you are your own definition of success, not someone else's.** Measure your success by comparing yourself to who you were yesterday, not who you wish to become tomorrow.
- **Hang out with people who support you, not those who put you down.** Remember the Law of Attraction. Surround yourself with positive people, people who believe in you, and soon you'll start believing in you too.
- **Remember that all those people you think are so much better than you ABSOLUTELY struggle with their own**

insecurities and private challenges. People are imperfect. That is the beauty of the human race. We always have lessons to learn and improvements to make.

FEAR OF NOT HAVING ENOUGH

Deep within our survival brain is the constant need to have enough resources to make it and ideally to live comfortably. We need enough money, a nice enough car, a large enough house, a good enough job, and we need enough time. We want to use ourselves to our full potential—that is what being a leader is about—and we may wonder: Am I using enough of my potential?

The fear of not having enough is a kind of "poverty mentality," which, although it began as a mindset about money, can affect our thinking in all areas of our life: You want to hold onto what you have because you fear you may not have enough in the future. This creates safety in your life but also leaves you open to missed opportunities. For instance, you may not risk taking some money out of savings to start your own business because you worry you might need that money in the future, even though you still have a safety net. Without taking that chance, things will likely stay the same when in fact you might have been capable of making far more money than what is in your savings account.

Overcoming the Fear of Not Having Enough:

1. **Imagine the worst-case scenario.** Often you'll discover that it's not so bad. If you don't pack enough clothes for a trip, you may have to go without clean clothes for a day or two, but that's not life threatening.

2. **Imagine the best-case scenario. Then make a plan.** This will put you in the right mindset to take a chance at making it happen, as long as you are willing to make sacrifices or compromises to mitigate negative outcomes. If you want to invest in a class or book about writing that great novel, adjust your meal budget for the next week or month so that you can make that purchase. You might discover that not only can you survive with less food but now you've put yourself one step closer to your dream of getting a novel published.

FEAR OF LOSS OF CONTROL

Do you worry that if you don't micromanage your life everything will fall apart? Do you fear losing control of your health, finances, marriage, children's happiness, and so forth? The fear of loss of control can create huge stress for many people, who may only get a brief intermission here and there from all their anxiety.

Let's face it: the world is always changing, and it's hard to meet a demand for certainty. You can't predict the future. You can only do your best to ensure that you are a success today and doing everything in your power to maintain your position.

Constantly worrying that you might lose control makes you a perfectionist in an imperfect world. It causes you to set very high, unrealistic demands that can never be met. Nothing will ever go exactly as you wish. Life is all about getting left curves and then getting past them.

Overcoming the Fear of Loss of Control:

The only way around this unrealistic need for control is to let go of your demand for certainty and perfectionism. If you can let go of the need to control the outcome, you are free to relax and enjoy life. Here are some ways to help you overcome this fear.

1. **Practice affirmations.** Say:
   "I refuse to live my life afraid of losing control."
   "I am good enough."
   "I don't have to be perfect."
   Think of it as a regular reminder to yourself that you are human, that you are a leader, and that leaders are human.

2. **Learn to live by probabilities, not guarantees.** Probabilities are only indications of how likely an outcome is, which can help you make an informed decision about your path. This is all we have in this wonderfully imperfect and unpredictable world. And this is all in your control!

So what's holding you back? Do you find it hard to lose weight? Do you dislike your body and avoid looking in the mirror? Do self-defeating thoughts keep you frozen and unable to make changes in your life? Do you feel overwhelmed by the stress in your life? You can change your life for the better and learn to love yourself by first recognizing your resistance and denial and then making your way toward commitment and confidence. I did it. And I'm going to help you get there.

The first step in reaching our potential is to stop doubting our potential. Give yourself a clean slate on which to begin charting those successes!

SUMMING UP

- Self-doubt and harmful self-talk are major problems holding people back. If we go into the world with our mind already clouded with negativity and fear, we're already setting ourselves up for failure. It's a self-fulfilling prophecy.
- Fear is part of being human. We all feel it at one time or another, but leaders are able to overcome their fears to achieve their goals.
- Fear of failure? Take a risk. Learn from every stumble. Nothing ventured, nothing gained.
- Fear of success? Use other leaders as models. Make a list of all the reasons why success frightens you, and use that to monitor your path toward your goals.
- Fear of rejection? Use the Progressive Overload method to overcome it: Brace the uncomfortable in small ways, and then slowly raise the stakes.
- Fear of not being enough? You ARE enough. Decide that. Memorize that. And keep your eyes on your own path, not somebody else's.
- Fear of not having enough? Try imagining both the worst- and best-case scenarios for following your goals. You'll often find what you want is more attainable than you think.
- Fear of loss of control? We live in an imperfect, mostly uncontrollable world. Let go of your demand for guarantees, and you'll free yourself to make informed decisions about the things you CAN control.

CHAPTER 5

THE POWER OF RELENTLESS OPTIMISM

"Whether you think you can or you think you can't, either way you are correct." —**HENRY FORD**

During the 1960s, Rubin "Hurricane" Carter, an American-Canadian boxer who was one of the top contenders for the middleweight title, was accused of triple homicide. The trial was biased, and Carter was convicted and awarded three life sentences, and yet he reported to prison in a tailored suit. Instead of giving in to his fate, he made it clear that "I am willing to stay here until I get out."

Carter refused to surrender to bogus judgment and spent every minute in prison studying law books and philosophy. It took almost nineteen years and two trials for the verdict to be overturned. And stepping out of the prison, Carter simply resumed his life as if nothing had happened.

This story made me change the way I think about each and every situation. I've been through numerous ups and downs in my life, and perhaps the toughest decision has been to choose whether I'd break or keep fighting.

What I've learned, though, is that the decision to keep fighting should be the easiest decision. Why? Because you should never give up. Because you are never completely powerless. No matter how tough the situation is, you are lucky to have your "powerful" mind to support you. And you need to use that power to think positively about the future and what's ahead of you.

MIRROR, MIRROR ON THE WALL...

To give you an idea of what happens to your body when you think like a victim or follower, try this simple exercise: Look in the mirror and think of a worst-case scenario. What happens to your facial expression? Most likely, you are frowning, eyebrows furrowed, shoulders tensed up, and hands clenched. And you are probably breathing quickly and shallowly. This is what worry does to you. Now take a deep breath, and think of something uplifting. Notice how quickly your expression changes, how your body relaxes. Your breathing is slow and deep, and you stand in front of the mirror, tall and confident. You have the power! You are strong! So act like it!

LEVERAGE POSITIVE EMOTIONS TO MASTER HEALTH

What are you thinking now? What were you thinking, say, five minutes ago? Ten minutes ago?

There's probably a constant war in your head, an ongoing dialogue between your inner self and your mind. *Am I good enough? Can I do it? Yes? No?* The voices inside your head are incredibly powerful and create your reality. They become your self-image and guide daily actions and decisions. You could say that the voices inside your head can create the story of your life.

A number of studies have shown that negative thinking— whether manifested as poor self-image, subclinical anxiety, or clinical depression—can adversely affect your health. But what about positive emotions? Can they actually make you healthier? According to Harvard School of Public Health professor Laura Kubzansky, the answer is yes. Research she conducted in 2007 found that participants with a positive outlook—what Kubzansky calls "emotional vitality," referring to those who generally expect outcomes in their favor—had a 20 percent reduction in heart diseases risk.[1]

American psychologist Martin E. P. Seligman, PhD, is the leading authority in the field of modern positive psychology. In his book *Learned Optimism: How to Change Your Mind and Your Life*, which discusses how optimism enhances quality of life, he writes:

> *The defining characteristic of pessimists is that they tend to believe that bad events will last a long time, will undermine everything they do, and are their own fault. The optimists, who are confronted with the same hard knocks of this world, think about misfortune in the opposite way. They tend to believe that defeat is just a temporary setback or a challenge, that its causes are just confined to this one case.*[2]

Other experts believe that the effect of positive thinking on health is indirect: Positive emotions may promote healthy behaviors, such as exercise, which leads to positive health outcomes. However, others, like Kubzansky, believe there is a direct effect, including improved sleep quality and perhaps even higher levels of antioxidants or good (HDL) cholesterol.

What this means for you is that, whatever the scientific reasoning, if you want to be a leader, you will have to ensure that your inner dialogue is mostly positive. You should be telling yourself things like:

- "I'm smart."
- "I'm interesting."
- "I go for what I want out of life."
- "I'm capable of doing what I need to do to get ahead."

On the other hand, if your inner voice is mostly negative—"I'm fat," "I'm stupid," "I'm clumsy," "I can never succeed"—you will not be able to tap into your body's capacity for good health, and, as a result, will sadly remain a victim for the rest of your life. What's worse is that you will feel powerless—you will assume that you have no control over your destiny when you most certainly do!

We've all heard of the saying that it's better to think of the glass as half full than half empty. I call that "relentless optimism." I always tell my clients that it's better to view life from a positive perspective than a negative one. I believe with all my heart that if you want to be a success in business, career, health and fitness, love, or ANYTHING really, you MUST have the ability to tap into optimism. If you fail to do so, you will unfortunately run back to your comfort zone when the tough times appear and in moments of extraordinary challenges.

"Watch your thoughts, for they become words. Watch your words, for they become action. Watch your actions, for they become habits. Watch your habits, for they become character. Watch your character, for it becomes your destiny."
—ANONYMOUS

•   •   •

ABUNDANCE THINKING VS. SCARCITY THINKING

Which one of the following would you say describes you best?

1. I scroll social media each day and feel jealous of friends who seem to lose weight so quickly and look great. It's not fair!
2. I scroll social media each day and am happy to root for my friends who look great and are trying to achieve their goals just as I am trying to achieve mine. We got this!

If you picked #2, congratulations! You are displaying an example of what's called "abundance thinking." People with this mindset view life through a positive prism and are ready for any challenges thrown their way as they march toward their goals. They also cheer on others' successes. If you display this type of thinking, you tend to focus on what you want to do and are not tied down by what's currently possible.

If you picked #1, you are displaying an example of "scarcity thinking," which I call a "not enough attitude." People with this mindset tend to complain about not having enough time, resources, money, or energy to achieve their goals. They focus on what's reasonable or comfortable and are envious of others' success. The concepts of abundance and scarcity as they relate to mindset were first put forward in author Stephen Covey's bestselling *The 7 Habits of Highly Effective People.*

In the desire for relentless optimism, having abundance thinking frees you up from negativity, whereas, sadly, a scarcity-based mindset only leaves you looking at what's bad and not working. The day you fuel your thoughts with abundance thinking, you will try everything and inch closer to success. Of course, abundance thinking does not *guarantee* success, but it ensures that you will keep trying even if something doesn't work out this time. You know that there is always a way, and it is just a matter of shuffling your strategy and trying again until you are able to find a way that actually works. Like with any skill, it can initially be challenging to maintain an abundance mindset at all times, but with consistent effort and determination you can make this your new default.

SCARCITY THINKING	ABUNDANCE THINKING
You feel there's never enough.	You feel there is always more.
You dislike sharing knowledge and helpful information with others.	You are happy to share your knowledge and experience with those around you.
It's hard to trust and build rapport with people.	You love interacting with people and can build rapport easily.
You dread competition.	You love competition and working on your skills.
You ask yourself, "How can I get away with less than expected?"	You ask yourself, "How can I give more than expected?"
You have a pessimistic outlook on most things.	You are optimistic and believe that the best is yet to come.
You feel there is nothing left to learn.	You are constantly seeking more knowledge and ways to improve.

FIXED VS. GROWTH MINDSET

Similar to the concept of abundance thinking vs. scarcity thinking, perhaps one of the most important life-changing concepts I've discovered is understanding the difference between a "growth mindset" and a "fixed mindset":

- **Growth mindset:** You believe that you can be good at anything because your abilities and skills depend entirely on your actions.
- **Fixed mindset:** You believe that your skills and talents are fixed based on your inherent nature because you're made that way.

This concept was introduced by world-renowned Stanford University psychologist Carol Dweck, who has spent decades researching achievement and success. Her research showed how a growth mindset that acknowledges the importance of effort creates motivation and leads to improved performance. Similarly, Stephen Covey stresses the importance of choosing a proactive rather than a reactive mindset and how hard work and good strategies can raise and improve personal talents, qualities, and attitudes.

By contrast, a fixed mindset is a common and harmful mindset. You can come up with hundreds of excuses why it is hard to stick to good habits or move out of your comfort zone. "I can't handle my business" is a classic example of a fixed mindset. It is a self-limiting belief that prevents important skills from developing. Meanwhile, people who have a growth mindset would be willing to run their business even if they failed at first. They are more willing to learn from failures and criticisms and to find inspiration rather than feeling threatened because they know they can learn and grow and improve their skill sets.

The biggest challenge plaguing those with a fixed mindset is often sitting right between their eyes! Yes, the stories they make up inside their head can either push them forward or prevent change from happening—there is a direct connection between what you *believe* and what you *do*. If you tell yourself "I'm not creative, it's hard for me to succeed," then it's pretty clear that you will not get very far and will feel like a failure. You will not feel like moving out of your comfort zone, and it will become almost impossible to get better.

If you are not happy or satisfied with your life, it's not because you are not as blessed as other people. It is because you've given up. If you want your career to improve or you want your personal relationships to progress a certain way, you must change your habits and overcome obstacles and challenges. You just have to be willing to open up your thinking and take the first step.

FIXED MINDSET	GROWTH MINDSET
You want to hide your flaws so that you are not judged by others.	You use your flaws as an opportunity to improve.
You stick with your comfort zone to keep up your fragile confidence.	You always push into an unfamiliar territory to make sure you are learning something new.
You let failures define you.	You believe that failures are only temporary setbacks.

GET OVER "BLACK AND WHITE" THINKING

People tend to have an all or nothing mindset. Black or white. Good or bad. Success or failure. "Everything in my life has to be perfect, or I'm a failure and people will see me as deficient and inadequate." In the quest for relentless optimism, this restrictive mindset will only set you up for frustration and failure and make it even harder to move forward. The truth is that nothing is black and white. We live in the gray areas of life, and they're messy, full of good and bad, successes and failures. Some things to keep in mind:

- **Remember that nothing is ever all bad or all good.** You have strengths and weaknesses. If you fail at one thing, it doesn't mean you are a failure.
- **When you catch yourself using the words "never" or "always," stop and ask yourself if what you're saying is true.** Could something "never" happen? Or "always" happen?
- **Ask yourself: "How can I view this differently, so it's not just either/or, black or white?"** This will help broaden your thinking to be open to an alternative viewpoint. Good leaders have a flexible mind.
- **Stop jumping to conclusions!** If someone didn't say hello to you while you were walking down the street, chances are it's not because he or she hates you. Maybe that person was preoccupied or shy or has poor vision and forgot to wear their glasses. Often we assume the intent of others without understanding what they are thinking or their motives for their actions. Don't let one bad incident define them—or you. Always keep an open mind and imagine other possibilities for someone else's behavior.

WHAT SUCCESSFUL LEADERS ALWAYS REMEMBER

- You have an infinite amount of talent. You don't know what you're good at until you try it! And there is always more to achieve in life, more to discover, and more to conquer.
- You don't have to achieve perfection. Being "perfect" is a false perception that we have taken on as our own often through viewing someone else's achievements or through media and movies. There is NO perfection; there is only incremental progress.
- There's absolutely no need to compete with others. Stop comparing yourself to others or their standards, and start focusing on yourself. There is always another level!
- The "I'm a loser" frame of mind pushes people away and, more importantly, repels resources you need to get what you want, further sabotaging your goals.

The power of relentless optimism has helped me become the man I am today—it gave me hope, inspired vision, and fuel for grit and determination. Without it, I would have given up on my dream of creating the Ultimate You Change Centers. I would have quit trying to get the six-pack I always wished for. And I would have even given up on writing this book to help inspire others to live an extraordinary life. About that I am POSITIVE!

Relentless optimism works! It's time to climb aboard the positivity train and speed toward your goals!

* * *

SUMMING UP

- Positive thinking is good for your health—physically and emotionally. Studies prove this. There really is no good reason NOT to think good thoughts!
- Optimism prepares you for life's inevitable stumbles. Leaders are happy not because they never fail; they're happy because they have EXPECTED to fail at some point, were ready for it, and have learned through failure better ways toward success.
- Abundance thinking focuses on possibilities rather than limitations, whereas scarcity thinking is focused on what you don't have.
- Those with a growth mindset believe their skill set is adaptable and improvable, that there's no stopping them when they put their mind to something. Those with a fixed mindset believe their skill set is innate and can't be improved.
- If you see life in terms of good and bad, pretty and ugly, fat and thin, success and failure, and all or nothing, then it's time for an attitude adjustment! There are no absolutes in life for leaders. Their yellow brick roads are paved in gray.

CHAPTER 6

HOW TO REPROGRAM YOUR MIND

"Life isn't about finding yourself. Life is about creating yourself." —GEORGE BERNARD SHAW

O ur brains are wonderful things. They are endlessly adaptable and dynamic. Brain plasticity, or neuroplasticity, is the brain's ability to change—via alterations in neural pathways and synapses—throughout our lives when it is exposed to new information from the environment, our experiences, our behaviors, etc. I'm not talking about some supernatural talent or abilities. Neuroplasticity is hardcore science! And how our brain decides to change depends largely on US! We CAN reprogram our minds.

How?

Through relentless optimism!

According to a research paper titled "The benefits of frequent positive affect: Does happiness lead to success?"[1] by psychology professors Laura King, Ed Deiner, and Sonja Lyubomirsky, the latter of whom wrote the bestseller *The How of Happiness: A New Approach to Getting the Life You Want*, the happiness-success link exists not only because success makes people happy but also because positive affect engenders success. Additionally, in another study titled "Pursuing happiness: The architecture of sustainable change,"[2] by Lyubomirsky, Kennon M. Sheldon, and David Schkade, the authors propose that a person's chronic happiness level is governed by three major factors: our genes, happiness-relevant circumstances, and, most importantly, our happiness-relevant activities and practices. What's more, the researchers believe that last category offers the BEST opportunity for sustainably increasing happiness!

Our thoughts release chemicals. When we're feeling happy, this positive mindset causes the brain to produce feel-good hormones, such as serotonin. And by practicing relentless optimism—saying things like "I am a winner!" or "I can do it!"—over time you consistently produce those hormones and strengthen those areas that stimulate positive feelings. Your mind and identity transform. You embrace life more joyfully, with hope, optimism, and good cheer. You enjoy better health, have happier relationships, and experience greater productivity in your career. And you have set the foundation to live a longer, more satisfying, and successful life.

"Imagination's everything. It is the preview of life's coming attractions." —ALBERT EINSTEIN

VISUALIZATION

In our quest to reprogram our minds, visualization is a powerful tool. Close your eyes and imagine biting into an apple. Did you salivate? There's a good chance you did. This is because the brain cannot distinguish an activity visualized from one that you actually perform, which means practicing with your mind and visualizing goals is as effective as practicing with your body.

This notion is backed up by a Bishop's University study conducted by Erin M. Shackell and Lionel G. Standing. The researchers, who reported their results in a paper titled "Mind Over Matter: Mental Training Increases Physical Strength,"[3] found that the brain patterns activated when a weightlifter lifts heavy weights are also similarly activated when the lifter just visualizes the act of lifting weights. What we focus on expands! Another example: Natan Sharansky, a computer specialist who spent nine years in prison in the USSR after being accused of spying for the US, said to himself, "I might as well use the opportunity to become the world champion!"[4] While in solitary confinement, Sharansky played mental chess with himself, and remarkably, in 1996, he beat world champion chess player Garry Kasparov!

Olympic athletes have been using visualization for years. This is why virtually all top performers in every profession—athletes, surgeons, musicians, actors, and business executives—perform actions in their mind before doing it in reality. Here are some examples of how celebrities have used visualization to improve their performances:

- Basketball legend Michael Jordan always pictured the last shot in his mind before he threw a hoop.
- Boxing legend Muhammad Ali pictured himself victorious long before the actual boxing match.
- Actor Jim Carrey used to picture himself as the greatest actor in the world when he was only a struggling actor.
- Arnold Schwarzenegger imagined his biceps to be mountain peaks as he pumped iron.

Take the time to use the power of your mind to create vivid images of your goal.

•   •   •

TIPS FOR VISUALIZING YOUR GOALS

Get detailed. The more vivid the details, the better the visualization will work for you. What type of clothes will you wear when you lose those fifty pounds? What will the standing ovation look like after you perform on stage? At first, it might take a bit of effort and time to fill in all the details the first time you envision the culmination of your goal, but when you revisit the image you will be able to call it up much more quickly. Also, picture in exquisite detail what you will do once your goal is reached. How great does it feel? How will this change your life? Repeat this process for all your goals.

Imagine every step. Your visualization should have a beginning and an end. If your goal is to learn to dunk a basketball, then you should visualize yourself not just at the hoop but from the moment you get the ball, every dribble down the court, the leap into the air, and, finally, the dunk itself.

Use all of your senses. Mental imagery is not only about vision but all five senses. What are you hearing? Smelling? Touching? If you want to live in a sprawling mansion on the ocean, see yourself lying on a cabana and hearing the *whoosh*, *whoosh* of the ocean surf at the shore. Feel the warm sun beating down on your face. Smell the fresh ocean air. Hear your children laughing as they build sandcastles. Feel your body surge with satisfaction for having achieved your goal.

Practice visualization daily. Ideally, shoot for ten to fifteen minutes a day of visualizing yourself achieving your goal. It'll take about twenty-one days for the practice to become routine.

OVERCOMING NEGATIVITY

How can we learn to feel more optimistic and limit negative thinking? Let's say you are working hard at building up your consulting business, but you keep running into obstacles. The following strategies will help you to take a more positive stance on your situation:

Develop a Positive Mantra.

A positive mantra is a powerful positive statement that you consciously choose to speak to empower yourself. When you say it, you help to restructure your brain to believe that anything is possible. For example, you repeat a mantra that states that your real self is healthy, wealthy, young, strong, powerful, loving, happy, and prosperous, or that you are the ultimate self-leader! Here are some examples of positive mantra:

I am strong.
I can handle anything.
I am a winner.
I am successful.
I am the master of my fate.
I attract fulfilling relationships.
I am loved.
I am wealthy.
I have a healthy and fit body.

When you keep repeating these positive and optimistic thoughts, you will have the energy and motivation to override the negative thoughts and move closer to success.

Find Evidence to Support
These More Resourceful Thoughts.

I am obsessed with reading biographies because they provide pages and pages of evidence that people can overcome obstacles and lead successful lives. They support my optimistic beliefs around what I want to accomplish, who I want to be, and where I want to take my life. The more you find evidence to support an optimistic thought, the more powerful it becomes.

Choose Gratitude.

Focus not on the things you don't have (scarcity thinking) but instead on all the gifts and awesomeness you do have. For example, you may not yet have enough money to take that trip around the world you've always dreamed of, but you have enough for a European vacation with your loved ones this year, and that's pretty amazing!

Eliminate Drama.

There's a lot of stress in life already. Don't add to it by having a meltdown, verbalizing drama, or having an overwhelming response every time things don't go your way. We need to be solution-focused leaders, not drama kings and queens!

Think of Setbacks as Challenges.

When an obstacle emerges in your path, think of it as an opportunity for personal growth. As Nietzsche said, "That which does not kill us makes us stronger." When you've made a poor choice with unfortunate consequences, don't demean yourself. Reflect on your choice, and learn from your mistakes. After all, learning from mistakes is one of the best assets of a leader.

Question EVERY Negative Thought.

Every time you are greeted by a negative thought or emotion, ask yourself, "How is this serving me?" If the emotion is of no use, toss it into the mental trash can and focus on things that are more important.

Don't Let Criticism Hijack a Compliment.

We have a tendency to magnify negative details. For instance, if someone admires our work and says something nice, "That painting was beautifully detailed. Nice job," but then says one small criticism, "Next time, add a bit more contrast in the background," we tend to focus on that negative detail and exclude the compliment. Some may even go to the extreme and dwell on it exclusively, letting it darken or distort their view of reality: "I am a lousy artist!" Try not to give these tiny criticisms more attention than they deserve!

Surround Yourself with Good Energy and Good People.

A positive environment is crucial for success, and who we choose to surround ourselves with determines how we feel and what we accomplish in life. Studies show that if we watch thirty minutes of sensationalized news stories or listen to a thirty-minute dose of complaining and gossiping with people around us, the effect on the brain is the same as if we had lived those experiences ourselves. The good news, according to psychologist Robert Sapolsky, who has studied a great deal about stress and the human brain, is that the negative effects of excessive stress can not only be stopped but also reversed. This is possible once the source of stress—psychological or physical—is removed or sufficiently reduced. You shouldn't feel sad about "deleting" negative people or situations from your life. That is your decision—in fact, it may be one of the best decisions you will ever make (for more on "Creating Your Success Environment," see Chapter 10).

Stop Giving Away Your Power.

When you're asked by family members or friends what you'd like to eat or what restaurant you'd like to visit or what movie you'd like to see, do you tend to say, "It doesn't matter—you pick"? Has letting others decide your fate become a habit? This might seem like a minor point, but it might be indicative of a major problem. You need to stop giving your power over to someone or something outside yourself and letting those exterior forces control the outcome. To become a leader, you must be in control of what happens to you.

Stop Blaming Others.

In addition to taking CONTROL of what happens to you, you also need to take RESPONSIBILITY for what happens to you. Do you find yourself blaming something or someone else for your problems? You might say, "It's not my fault that I didn't finish the project on time. My boss gave me too much work." Or, "I only ate the whole cake because my husband put it in front of my face." Or, "He makes me nervous." Or, "She made me do it." You need to stop playing the "victim." Blaming others will only keep you locked into making poor choices. Embrace the philosophy that YOU MAKE things happen, rather than believing that life is happening to you. You must believe that you are the captain of your ship, the master of your fate, and that achievements, relationships, health, and physical fitness are in your control.

REPROGRAMMING ON THE GO

- Is there traffic on the road? Is the rain spoiling your outdoor event? Think of every obstacle in your path as an opportunity for personal growth. Maybe the traffic will allow you to listen to that podcast you've been meaning to check out. Maybe the rain will cool down the air and provide a respite from the heat. Look for the silver lining in every cloud, even if it's a rain cloud!
- When things don't go your way, think of experiences and situations where you were successful to help change your mood.
- When complimented, get in the habit of saying, "Thank you," rather than refuting the compliment.
- Jot down your negatives. After all, we all have them! Next to each, write a personal strength, accomplishment, or behaviour.
- Practice self-compassion, and treat yourself to the same kindness and compassion that you would to a true friend or to a child in a similar situation.
- Ask better questions like, "If this situation is here to teach me a positive lesson, what is it teaching me?"

THE POWER OF MANTRAS AND AFFIRMATIONS

Celebrities are often known for using affirmations in order to live high-profile, successful lives. I have spoken to many incredible athletes and entrepreneurs on the topic of positive mantra, and ALL OF THEM use affirmations, whether they openly speak about it or not. When interviewing Olympic gold medallist Cathy Free-man on my show, she spoke to me about the affirmation she has used daily since the age of ten: "I am the greatest athlete in the world." Day in and day out she would use this affirmation or man-tra, and the rest they say is history! The following three celebrities also have been vocal about using them to manifest their needs and bring positive and permanent change to their lives:

- **Jim Carrey:** Comedian Jim Carrey has long told stories of his rise to fame, and one of the most famous ones he's shared was how in the early 1990s he wrote a check to himself in the amount of $10 million for "acting services rendered." He postdated the check for Thanksgiving 1995 and carried it in his wallet. Carrey also visualized himself cashing the check and what he would buy with it. Just before Thanksgiving 1995, he found out he would be making $10 million on the film *Dumb and Dumber*. He was indeed wealthy enough to cash the check!
- **Will Smith:** Actor Will Smith is one of the highest paid actors in Hollywood, with a positive attitude that has been his trademark for years. In interviews, he has spoken of his need to connect with the universe and that he believes that people control their own destiny. In an interview to promote his movie the *Pursuit of Happiness*, Smith said,

> *The idea is that you have command over what your future, what your situation is. That you internally and with your spirit or however you want to put it— the Tao or Muslim Allah or Jesus, whatever that uni-versal force is that you connect to—you, in sync with that force, have command to will your future.*[5]

- **Oprah Winfrey:** Oprah Winfrey, who pulled herself up from poverty to become one of the wealthiest women in the world, is quite vocal about using positive affirmations. "You really can change your own reality based on the way that you think," she told host Larry King back in a 2007 interview. Her commitment started young as she watched her grandmother toil away on a farm. Winfrey—who has discussed creating her own vision boards to realize her dreams—once said in an interview that she had been watching her grandmother boil clothing in a big iron pot (they didn't have washing machines at the time), and she remembers telling herself over and over again, "My life won't be like this, my life won't be like this, it will be better." She has advised fans to "create the highest, grandest vision possible for your life, because you become what you believe."[6]

LIVING IN THE NOW

"Life can be found only in the present moment.
The past is gone, the future is not here, and if we do
not go back to ourselves in the present moment, we
cannot be in touch with life." —**THICH NHAT HANH**

One of the very best ways to gain control over your thoughts and become optimistic is by practicing mindfulness meditation. Mindfulness meditation involves purposefully paying attention to the present, neutrally and nonjudgmentally, and the benefits are immense—physically, mentally, and spiritually! Life can be found only in the present moment. Yet, most of us live our lives controlled by past and future thoughts. If you learn to focus your attention on what is happening now, you can learn to take control of your thoughts.

Here are a few tips for incorporating mindfulness meditation into everyday life:

- Wherever you are—standing in line at the supermarket, filling up the gas tank—become aware of your body. Notice how you are breathing, how you are standing, how relaxed or tense your muscles are.
- Wherever you are, become aware of your surroundings. Feel the warmth of the sun on your face. Feel the wind brushing against your face. Listen to the birds chirping and the rustling of the squirrel running up the tree.
- When thoughts enter your mind, accept and observe them neutrally, and then let them go. Learning how to do this will take time and work, but it will happen if you make mindfulness a way of life. You can start with a short, five-minute meditation session each day and gradually increase the time as you get more competent and confident.

Reprogramming your mind won't happen overnight, but rarely anything worth doing does. Luckily, our brains allow us to try a little bit every day to become better people, to get stronger and stronger. And if we can try to get rid of all those negative thoughts, over time they will slowly diminish and be replaced by more rational, balanced thinking.

I often say, "The quality of your life will be determined by the quality of questions you ask yourself daily." In moments of stress, negativity, or drama, I want you to get better at asking quality, powerful questions that allow you to take something of value away from every single experience in life, good or bad. These are my two favorite reframing questions:

- If this were a gift, what would it be giving me?
- If this were a lesson, what would I be learning?

These questions have helped me learn thousands of priceless lessons, and I hope they do the same for you.

You have the power to reprogram your mind and change your thinking. Remember, it took you your whole life to learn how you think today. Now it's time to learn a more rewarding and resourceful way for tomorrow. Experience small pleasures every chance you get, and soon you will see big changes in your mindset!

SUMMING UP

- We have the power to change the way our brains function. Thanks to neuroplasticity, our brains have the ability to reorganize themselves and adapt to new behaviors.
- The practice of visualization lets us dream it till we live it. Seeing is believing!
- To overcome negative thinking, practice mantras, read books about leaders and success, be thankful, eliminate drama, view obstacles as challenges, don't let criticism hijack a compliment, surround yourself with good people, and take ownership of thoughts and behaviors.
- Positive mantras and affirmations have been used by many celebrities and successful people to make their dreams a reality.
- To achieve peace of mind, practice mindfulness meditation and use reframing questions during moments of stress.

CHAPTER 7

NONNEGOTIABLE SUCCESS CHARACTERISTICS

"Don't worry about what the world needs.
Ask what makes you come alive and do that, because
what the world needs is people who have come alive."
—HOWARD THURMAN

Every person you come across views success differently. Some see it as being able to run a mile; others see it as being able to run twenty-six miles. Some see it as becoming a chef or opening a fancy restaurant; others view it as being able to cook dinner each night for their family at home. So what exactly is the recipe for success? Well, there really is no perfect recipe, but the following are seven ingredients that combine well, in varying amounts, in virtually all successful people.

. . .

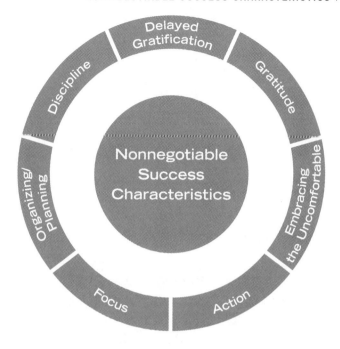

1. SELF-DISCIPLINE

Self-discipline is a conscious effort to succeed, every day, despite self-doubt. It involves giving up things that you want, like time with friends and family, or money to go to the pub, to achieve your larger goals. People with self-discipline do what is best for them even when they don't feel like it. More importantly, they know how to get through the tasks they've chosen for themselves without making excuses.

Example: American businessman Jack Welch, the former chairman and CEO of General Electric, started from the bottom and worked his way to the top of the food chain in the corporate world using his determination and self-discipline. As a hard-working kid in Massachusetts, Welch worked summers as a golf caddie or a newspaper boy or a shoe salesman, and he eventually graduated from college with a Master's in chemical engineering. When he joined GE in 1960, his salary was just over $10,000. He worked his way up and, in 1981, became GE's youngest chairman and CEO.

How I do it: Initially, I couldn't talk to strangers but pushed through my discomfort and tried a little bit each day. I knew I had to if I wanted to achieve my goals of building my business. Now, I am surrounded by huge numbers of excited clients.

How you can too: If you lack self-discipline big time, try using the strategy of Progressive Overload that we talked about in Chapter 4 (see page 42). Dedicate small chunks of time—every day—to whatever new thing you are doing or goal you want to achieve. Gradually, every few days, increase the amount of time you spend doing it. This strategy will help you adapt to the activity and will strengthen your discipline muscle, creating better habits.

2. GRATITUDE

We talked a bit about gratitude in Chapter 6 as a way of becoming a better version of ourselves. Being thankful is important in creating success, not just happiness. Even gratitude for failure is important, which reveals to us what parts of ourselves, our strategies, and our training need to be improved. Learning to appreciate the small wins and losses along the way is necessary as a means of keeping us motivated.

Example: American author and life coach Tony Robbins lives and breathes gratitude in his life and businesses, and, through this, he is able to control his emotional state as well as empower his teams. Each day, Robbins takes time to focus on three moments in his life that he's grateful for. Why? "Gratitude is the antidote to the things that mess us up," he says. "You can't be angry and grateful simultaneously. You can't be fearful and grateful simultaneously."[1]

How I do it: Following Robbins's lead, every night my beautiful wife and I have made a commitment to say three things we are grateful for from the day that just passed. It's such a great way to end the day by appreciating what you have and the experiences you live.

How you can too: Join us! Take a moment to think about what you're thankful for. Make it a daily habit.

3. EMBRACING THE UNCOMFORTABLE

Growth is done outside of our comfort zone. If something doesn't challenge you, it doesn't change you. You need to be actively seeking out challenges and situations where you are uncertain whether or not you will win, and you need to train yourself to give 100 percent effort with confidence, even if the odds look stacked against you. When you are always tackling goals, winning becomes an instinct, and, with previous successes behind you, you gain momentum and you are able to dream bigger and set the bar higher.

Example: Technology entrepreneur Elon Musk has some great stories of utilizing this trait, especially when his companies were about to collapse during the economic downturn! Whether it's taking on a demanding self-learning spree in the fields of rocket science and space technology in order to build his knowledge and lead his team at SpaceX or working around the clock for more than a month when Tesla needed an infusion of capital,[2] Musk hustles and is always trying new ways to move forward.

How I do it: This characteristic is so important to me on a personal level; it is probably the one that has helped me grow the most in life. I truly respect it and love it—so much so that I have "Be Uncomfortable" tattooed on my wrist as a constant reminder to never slip into complacency. If I ever feel myself sliding in that direction, I look down at my wrist and swiftly give myself a kick in the ass and then get back to pursuing my purpose.

How you can too: Think about the way babies learn new things, such as trying to stand. It's difficult. And uncomfortable. Even though they keep falling, they change their stance each time until they are able to stay up a bit longer. They keep trying until they discover what works and they are able to walk without help. Embrace the uncomfortable by approaching whatever it is again and again, in new ways, until it gets easier and easier.

4. ORGANIZATION AND PLANNING

Do you feel that there aren't enough hours in the day to get everything done on your to-do list? At the same time, do you find yourself spending more time on little things than on the important work in your life? What's more, do you often fail to take time for pleasure and relaxation and crawl into bed stressed and exhausted? If you live in today's modern society, most likely the answer is "yes" to all three. You can turn things around by learning how to manage your time rather than have your time manage you.

Example: In 1987, Howard Schultz acquired the Starbucks coffee brand and began what would become one of the most ambitious expansions in retail history! He took Starbucks from one location to 26,000 globally through careful organization and planning of every facet of the company—right down to the exotic, Italian-inspired "grande" and "venti" sizes of its coffee.[3] To achieve a feat like that is intense and beautiful!

How I do it: Now this is something that I struggled with growing up and one that I really had to amplify my focus on to not only master but appreciate. I do this by organizing my day into manageable, focused blocks of time that include carefully scheduled healthy meal breaks and exercise.

How you can too: By having a plan and sticking to it, you can work toward your goals and objectives. Prioritize your to-do list, and invest your time in activities that matter the most, making sure you make time for yourself too. There are many ways to do this. Have you heard of the 1–3–5 strategy? Organize each day around one big thing, three medium things, and five small things. I'm also a big fan of "eating your frog," a term coined by bestselling author Brian Tracy that means you should tackle your first major task each morning as a way to reach high levels of performance daily. (The term is based on an old saying that if the first thing you do each morning is eat a live frog, then you'll have the satisfaction of knowing that that will probably be the worst thing you do that day.)

•　　•　　•

5. DELAYED GRATIFICATION

I remember a conversation I had with one of my amazing mentors, author Sharon Pearson. I was telling her about what I had accomplished and sacrificed, and she stopped me and said, "Good. Keep sacrificing for the next ten years, and then just maybe your business will become the success you want to be!"

As a society, we are guilty of constantly chasing instant gratification—the desire to experience pleasure or fulfillment RIGHT NOW. You get the urge to eat a tub of ice cream, and you do it! You see a pair of new shoes at the mall, and you must have them! You know you should stay in and focus on your project or business this weekend, but friends talk you into going out and getting hammered. ALERT: Instant gratification!

Let me tell you a secret: Instant gratification is a trick, a distraction to keep you stuck, average, and mediocre. If you have big dreams, then living for instant gratification is a sucker's game. You need to focus on DELAYED gratification—working and waiting for the things you really want. You see, people run from delayed gratification because the thought of a little sacrifice in the present seems like too much effort or pain, but people don't realize that in that moment of instant pleasure they are conditioning a terrible behavior that will bring on only more of what they already have: shitty results!

Example: Chinese businessman and philanthropist Jack Ma, cofounder and executive chairman of technology conglomerate Alibaba Group and one of the richest men in the world, bootstrapped his whole business. Ma grew up poor in communist China, failed his university entrance exam TWICE, and was rejected from lots of jobs.[4] But that didn't stop him! Four years after his first two ventures failed, he gathered about twenty friends in his apartment and convinced them to invest in a vision he had for Alibaba. He made it a habit to delay gratification, especially through the start of his business career, so he could spend more time on work and more money on his business and make it a success!

How I do it: When I committed to my vision and my future self, I stopped going out and partying. I stopped spending money on rubbish and wasting time on things that did not add value to my mission. With every decision I made, I asked this question: *Is this going to get me closer to my goal or further away?* If the answer was the latter, then I knew I had to make a better decision; otherwise, I was selling myself short and compromising my dreams.

How you can too: Have the courage to say no to temptation. Too many people aren't willing to give up on partying, their poor diet, and bad influences. I often wonder about people who are out getting drunk all the time and then complain about how much their life sucks. I want to ask them: "What the hell are you celebrating when you party? Being broke and unhappy?" Of course, they are using it as an escape. Things like junk food, drugs, gambling, etc., are like a sedative that takes away from your life without giving anything back in return. I urge you to be smart about this. If you want a different result in life, then you need to be willing to behave differently, act differently, and make decisions differently. If you want success, then you have to be willing to work and WAIT for it.

6. ACTION

Leaders are persistent—they take action when presented with a choice or crossroads. They pivot when necessary. They have "grit"—

they stick to a task until it is completed, no matter how long it takes. They don't give up easily. Gritty people strive for excellence, assuming an attitude that allows for failure, disappointment, and vulnerability in the quest for improvement and reaching their goal.

Example: English business magnate Richard Branson, the founder of the Virgin Group, is always on the move. He is a great example of a leader who sees opportunity and takes massive action, such as when he sold Virgin Records and decided to buy Virgin Atlantic Airways.

How I do it: Every day, taking action is crucial. It could be seeing a standard drop in the team and having to correct it or move a team member on. It could be a drop in sales and having to rectify sales and cash flow. It could be seeing a drop in leads or marketing flow and having to regain momentum. In business, we don't have the luxury of waiting things out. Massive action is always a MUST.

How you can too: Answer every call to action. And if there is no call, research and practice skills so that you're prepared when there is. Also, action can be about celebrating every small win and incremental improvement along your journey. For example, writing a book sometimes takes years to achieve. Celebrate the completion of each chapter instead of waiting until the end of your goal.

7. FOCUS

Focus and concentration have become a real challenge in this age of constant distraction, especially when you have to face a daily bombardment of emails, text messages, and audio- visual stimulation. You need to take 100 percent responsibility for eliminating the distractions in your life if you truly want to WIN!

Example: American computer pioneer Steve Jobs, the chairman, CEO and cofounder of Apple, was famous for his laser focus on simplicity and eliminating products that would distract from his company's core offering. "Focusing is about saying no," Jobs once said. "And the result of that focus is gonna be some really great products where the total is much greater than the sum of the parts."[5]

How I do it: As I write this book, I could easily let myself get distracted and jump on Facebook and scroll for hours on end, shop on Amazon, or jump on my phone and watch Netflix, but I know that if I do that I'm feeding into a weakness, an emotional complacency that if nurtured only grows more fierce and needy every day. Instead, I start to create an awareness around this, a mindfulness that allows me to concentrate on what is important and ignore the "noise" so that I can commit to the success that is waiting to be unleashed!

How you can too: Think about the distractions that suck up your time and focus—your phone, social media like Facebook and Twitter, emails, friends calling, the TV…The list goes on. A tried-and-true solution to remaining focused is to get RID of the things that pull you away from purposeful activities and train your brain to pay complete attention to the present moment. Start by practicing the mindfulness exercises that we discussed in Chapter 6.

Leaders don't only look forward. They look at themselves. Are you the person today that you want to be tomorrow?

· · ·

SUMMING UP

- Success has different meanings for different people. The path to your goals will not look like anyone else's.
- There is no recipe for greatness. Success is what you make of it, although leaders tend to share certain characteristics.
- The seven nonnegotiable characteristics that leaders have include: self-discipline, gratitude, embracing the uncomfortable, organization and planning, delayed gratification, action, and focus.

PART 3

TAKE ACTION

CHAPTER 8

THE MOTIVATION MATRIX

*"Success is not the key to happiness. Happiness is
the key to success. If you love what you are doing,
you will be successful."* —**ALBERT SCHWEITZER**

D o you start things and never follow through and finish them?
Do you waste days and weeks procrastinating? That's okay,
because it's completely normal and common. You don't need to be
in despair for not having the motivation you've needed in the past.
Your past does not equal your future.

Motivation is a learned behavior. It is not some special unicorn
that is mystical and that only the lucky few high performers inher-
ently have. If you put effort and time into developing your motivation, you can create the same results as other successful people.

Anyone who has set personal goals knows that goal setting,
alone, doesn't always guarantee success. It is only the first step in a
long process. Then you need to work hard for the second step—ac-
tivation—and you need something to get you there. That's where
motivation comes in.

There are two main types of motivation: extrinsic and intrinsic.
Extrinsic motivation is due to external factors. For example, if you
are studying hard to please your parents or you are working hard

to put food on the table for your family, it is due to extrinsic motivation.

Intrinsic motivation, on the other hand, is due to internal factors—i.e., you have personal motivation or reasons to perform a particular task. For example, you get up early in the morning to hit the gym or stroll into Ultimate You to get a workout done on the green because you want to get fit and be the best version of you. Or you are eager to get up, dress up, and leave for work because you want to make money—another big motivator in life! You may not be able to control the external factors happening in your life, but you do have absolute control over the thoughts and action you take each day.

When I thought about starting Ultimate You Change Centers, I penned down my ideas and also my personal motivators for each. I found that there were three major elements that made up personal motivation:

- **Desire:** You need to have a strong personal desire to meet a particular goal or objective.
- **Commitment:** There has to be strong commitment followed by the willingness and readiness to act on the opportunities and make them work in your favor.
- **Tenacity:** You need to have the ability to keep going and pursue your goals even if you face obstacles or setbacks.

Imagine how much you would achieve if you had unlimited motivation. If you could resist the temptation to procrastinate! Motivation is the creator of every goal—it builds empires, it takes people to the moon—and will be responsible for everything great you achieve in life! So we need to master the art of staying motivated.

What if I told you there was a method that would allow you to gain and utilize extreme motivation to attack your goals with no hesitation and no procrastination? There is! I call it the Motivation Matrix, and it includes five important components: "CHANGE" goals, Pain Stacking, Pleasure Stacking, Accountability Stacking, and a Strategy for Setbacks.

A WORD ABOUT DESPERATION AS MOTIVATION

I often meet people who are "desperate" to make changes in their life. They've hit rock bottom. Have nowhere else to turn. Remember my friend Stephen? Although it is best to make changes in our lives BEFORE we reach the point of desperation, because then we're making those changes from a place of calm and reason, if you find yourself desperate to make a change, use this energy as FUEL. Too often we associate desperation with "panic" or fear, but we can see it as more of a positive thing—a launch pad. So if you feel desperate right now, that is fine—in fact, that is great. It means that you have momentum behind you and the energy to start making real changes. After all, you are reading this, and that's a good sign.

1. "CHANGE" GOALS

People are creatures of habit and comfort, for the most part. We generally do what is easiest, and usually by default, unless taught otherwise—we are not long-term oriented. If this weren't true, obesity and overspending would not be real first-world problems. We know we shouldn't eat bad foods or smoke cigarettes, but we find temporary comfort in these things. When establishing goals, we need to ask ourselves: Is the juice worth the squeeze? Is the effort or discomfort worth the result? If the answer is yes, if your why is big enough, you will always be motivated.

Remember the characteristics of the "CHANGE" goals we talked about in Chapter 3:

- (C)HALLENGING
- (H)EARTFELT
- (A)CTIONABLE WITH A DEADLINE
- (N)ONNEGOTIABLE
- (G)REATER GOOD
- (E)XACT

Think of a goal that incorporates all of these characteristics. When selecting a goal, you need to see the value in the goal, not just in one area of life but in multiple areas. You need to connect the dots and start to amplify the pleasure and value that achieving this thing is going to have on your life! Go through the "CHANGE" goal criteria and really try to get your goals in alignment with it. Now input this goal into the matrix below (I usually have a maximum of three goals per matrix), and let's begin filling in your motivational strategy.

THE MOTIVATIONAL TRAP

There is a trap when setting goals. If your goals are not truly meaningful to you, then as soon as you face adversity, you will give into distractions and instant gratification. Similarly, if you are focusing on just a single element of your goal, the momentum and motivation behind you will be minimal. Having goals that perhaps don't feel meaningful enough to you—such as getting a six-pack and only a six-pack—will likely cause you to give up in the face of inconveniences or plateaus. We need to focus on the greater vision—the impact our goals will have on our lives and on the people around us. That's what makes "CHANGE" goals so effective.

1. CHANGE GOAL

2. STRATEGY FOR SETBACKS

Potential setbacks:

Corresponding strategies:

3. PLEASURE STACK

4. PAIN STACK

5. ACCOUNTABILITY STACK

Accountability to yourself:

Accountability to another:

Accountability to a group:

2. PLEASURE STACKING

Pleasure stacking involves writing down all the positive consequences you strive for and want to achieve with your goal in your
Motivation Matrix. (Just the act of doing that will feel great!)

For instance, if your goal is to lose weight, you need to create
layers and reasons as to why this is such a positive goal. This helps
to protect your goal and inspire yourself to make greater change.
How will losing weight affect your relationships? Will it make you
happier, more attractive, and easier for you to find partners that you
want? Will it add more passion to your relationships? Ask yourself:

- Will it affect my vitality and zest for life?
- Will it affect my self-worth and energy levels?
- What will people be saying about me? How will it make
  me feel?

The more pleasures you can stack, the more inspired you will be,
and the less likely you will give into instant gratification or pressure
on the days you want to give up on your goals and dreams.

Take this exercise a step further and consider how it will impact
different areas of your life. How will achieving this goal affect your:

- Social time?
- Finances?
- Career or business?
- Learning and education?
- Ability to contribute?
- Health and vitality?
- Family and relationships?

If you ask yourself these questions, you will find inspiration and
positive emotions to really know deep down why your goals matter

and why achieving what you want is really nonnegotiable. Put the time in to make this list as large as possible, and optimize the list daily or weekly. The more reasons you can make, the more emotional leverage you can utilize to create lasting motivation.

DOING WHAT YOU LOVE

We have a tendency to have better motivation when we love, or have a passion for, our goals. If Malcolm Gladwell is right that "ten thousand hours is the magic number of greatness," as he wrote in his 2008 book *Outliers: The Story of Success*, then it makes sense to love what you do—after all, you're going to be spending a lot of time doing it! What's more, studies show that it's easier to cope with stress and even long working hours if you enjoy the work you are doing[1]—there is a positive correlation between job productivity and job satisfaction.

PAIN STACKING

The same way there is pleasure stacking as a motivating force in our Motivational Matrix, there is also pain stacking. Pain stacking is leveraging the emotional powers of ideas, reasons, fears, and outcomes if you do NOT take action or change.

For instance, it could be:

- "If I don't lose weight, I might not be alive for my daughter's wedding."
- "If I don't make the effort to be social and go on dates, I might not find the one."

- "If I don't help myself, I can't help others, I can't donate to people in need, and I can't inspire the people around me."

Ask yourself: "If I don't become motivated, focused, and committed to my goals, where will I be in five years from now if I don't change?" How will it affect my:

- Social time?
- Finances?
- Career or business?
- Learning and education?
- Ability to contribute?
- Health and vitality?
- Family and relationships?

Jot down your answers. Again, we are leveraging the emotions from our foresight. And through this we can protect ourselves from being lazy and passive about our dreams and goals.

ACCOUNTABILITY STACKING

On the journey to achieve your goals, accountability is going to be your friend. Accountability is an *obligation*—of you or of someone else—to "account" for your activities, to take responsibility for them, and, usually, to disclose the results in a timely and consistent manner. There are different types of accountability:

- **Level 1: Promise yourself that you are going to take action or make a change.** Unless you have gone through life setting goals and hitting them every single time, you have to focus on personal accountability. Take this very seriously because if you can't stick to promises you make to yourself, you won't trust yourself and be confident when setting new goals later. Treat personal accountability as life or death—your vision depends on it!

- **Level 2: Tell a close friend about your new goal.** Humans have an inherent trait of finding it important to stick to what we said we would commit to. This adds to the pressure to keep your word. Research has shown that publicly committing to a goal to someone gives you at least a 65 percent change of completing it. And having a SPECIFIC accountability partner increases your chance of success to 95 percent![2] Leverage this! And be sure to choose a friend that you know will call you up if you don't follow through.
- **Level 3: Tell a mentor, teacher, or someone you respect greatly or look up to about your goal.** This person may provide you with a stronger level of accountability than anyone else because you would feel bad or embarrassed to let him or her down.
- **Level 4: Tell a community or group of like-minded people about your new commitment.** Not only does this provide you with more than one accountability partner but it offers a built-in cheerleading section!

PLANNING FOR SETBACKS

There are going to be times when we are tired and our willpower has been depleted. If you can plan for those times, for those set-backs, you can maintain your upward spiral. For instance, if you are out with your mates or you are going somewhere where you are not sure you can find a healthy meal, prepare something in advance and bring it with you. A solution-focused mindset will help you maintain your motivation. Consider what could be a possible and realistic setback on your journey, and then have an action plan to deal with it—rather than waiting until they happen. If you can't come up with a solution to a potential problem, speak to someone who has been where you want to go—no matter how obscure you think your problem is, someone has probably been there. And if you can't find someone, let Google be your friend.

At this point, your Motivation Matrix should be nice and full and might look something like the one on page 95.

●   ●   ●

Motivation can breathe fresh air into your old, stagnant goals. If you are still struggling to find yours, here are two last pieces of advice to consider:

1. **Stop overthinking.** A great deal of complications and chaos in our life is because of unwanted analysis we do as adults. Sometimes you will ask yourself all sorts of questions, and some of them won't be needed in the first place. I can recall countless nights when I was lying awake and wrestling with my brain. I was trying so hard to figure out what I want to do in life, and there were days I was exhausted even before I began. Thankfully, I realized that all this overthinking was not leading me anywhere. I could not predict the future, but, deep down, I knew what choices mattered the most to me.

2. **Don't expect miracles to happen.** We've all heard the saying that we should "be ready when opportunity knocks," but far too many people are sitting around and *waiting* for opportunity to knock. You might be the best singer in the world, but *American Idol* isn't going to come knocking on your door. You have to be out there performing and taking action.

1. CHANGE GOAL

Step 1: Write down your CHANGE Goal.

I will complete a fitness challenge (9in6) by December 30, this year, to prepare for our family hike in Tasmania.

2. STRATEGY FOR SETBACKS

Step 2a: Write down any potential setbacks that will take you off track from your goals.

Step 2b: Write down strategies to handle these setbacks and make sure you get back on track.

Potential setbacks:	Corresponding strategies:
· It's too cold! · I keep hitting the snooze button and then miss classes because I'm late. · I have a wedding coming up. · Work gets really busy this time of the year.	· Turn heater on with timer and dress warmly. · Pack my gym back the night before, get to bed early, have my alarm on other side of bedroom. · Eat my meals before wedding, eat only what's on plan, and have meal ready when I get home. · Get work out in early in the morning so it's done.

3. PLEASURE STACK

4. PAIN STACK

Step 3: Write down the tangible benefits and rewards and the positive emotions you'll feel as a result of achieving your CHANGE Goal.

Step 4: Write down the painful consequences and the negative emotions you'll feel as a result of NOT achieving your CHANGE Goal.

· *I'll have finished my first fitness challenge and get back the motivation I've been lacking all these years. I'll feel a sense of pride for getting it done.*
· *I'll get healthier, fitter and stronger which will build on my confidence so that I can be an even more awesome version of me!*
· *I'll spend quality time with my family when we go to Tassie. Which means I can connect with my partner and kids so much more. I know this will make me and the whole family so much happier.*

· *I'll waste more of my time, my years, my energy and money getting unfit and lazy. I'll never get motivated and I'll always feel slobbish and disappointed in me.*
· *I'll get weaker and fatter and more unhealthy, which would make me feel depressed, and that would raise my chances of an early death.*
· *I'll disappoint my family and will gradually lose them, as I set a bad example. My kids won't look up to me anymore, and my partner won't find me attractive. I'll let my family down, and that would kill me!*

5. ACCOUNTABILITY STACK

Step 5: Stack your accountability in 3 different ways.

Accountability to yourself:	Accountability to another:	Accountability to a group:
Write a signed letter or contract to yourself.	*Tell a mentor, best friend about what you're working to achieve.*	*Tell a group or community (e.g., Facebook) what you're working to achieve.*

If I look back at my life today, I would find that the paths leading me to where I am presented me with a scary picture at first. I could have easily spun down the spiral of anxiety, but I knew I needed to find my motivation. I didn't want to feel hopeless. I'm a warrior, NOT a worrier! I knew it was only me who could make my life better. Every step of my journey wasn't the easiest, and there was no one to help me discover exactly what I was meant to do, but I thought it through. I tried and failed and tried again.

While I can never really know how the next few years will go line by line, what I do know is that I will be working, pushing, fighting, loving, and challenging myself 100 percent to make my vision a reality. My personal motivation strategy fuels my success and asskickery daily. And yours can too.

Battles are won and lost in the mind. Become the master of motivation, and you'll leverage your emotions for the right actions.

SUMMING UP

- Motivation is the key to jumpstarting your goals. It is the vital link between goal setting and action.
- Motivation can be extrinsic or intrinsic, and it requires intense desire, commitment, and tenacity. This makes it very important to consider the positive impact your goals will have on others and on various parts of your life.
- The Motivation Matrix will help you keep track of your goals and plan for setbacks. It consists of five main elements: "CHANGE" goals, Pleasure Stacking, Pain Stacking, Accountability Stacking, and a Strategy for Setbacks.
- To stay motivated, avoid overthinking and waiting for opportunity to knock on your door. Action is required.

CHAPTER 9

BUILDING GOOD HABITS

"Let our advance worrying become advance thinking and planning." —**WINSTON CHURCHILL**

W hat truly separates the greats from the average? The 1 percent from the 99 percent? The people who consistently get results every single day from the people who struggle to achieve their goals and dreams? It's a person's habits.

Habits are the rituals and processes we take part in on a daily and weekly basis. They are things that are automatic for us. Generally, there are two types of habits:

- **Resourceful habits:** Those that help us move closer to our dreams, like always making the choice to take the stairs for exercise instead of the elevator.
- **Unresourceful habits:** Those that are detrimental to our goals, health, wealth, and happiness, like that little habit of getting a chocolate bar every time you go through the checkout.

In your own life, look at your own habits, and ask yourself: Do they move you closer to your goal or do they hinder your chances of reaching your goal?

THE BIG POWER OF SUBTLE HABITS

How do you start your day? What subtle habits and rituals do you run at night before bed? We all have things we do every day. We get up. We get dressed. We brush our teeth. We eat breakfast. Feed the dog or cat. Water the plants. We go to the gym. We read bedtime stories to our children. And all these things affect our mindset, our life, our capacity for doing and being. Does it help you to get amazing sleep so you are ready to unleash the next day? Or do your thoughts keep you up at night affecting the next day's performance?

These little choices have a compounding effect that we often do not pay attention to. For example, a sugar addiction is a real thing—studies show that its affect on the brain is similar to opiates[1]—that many people are unaware they even have. According to the American Heart Association, many people consume more sugar than they realize: Men and women should have no more than nine and six teaspoons a day, respectively,[2] but the average American adult has twenty-two teaspoons per day![3]

Deep down, we know we are better off always saying no to that chocolate bar and that with time—usually fourteen days off sugar—our cravings will lessen. That chocolate bar could also lead to you having allergies later that day or a drop in energy, confidence, and clarity, and then suddenly you make a bad first impression for a job interview or you just feel crappy for the rest of the day.

Most people live in denial, never paying attention to how these little habits and rituals we have and repeat unconsciously can have dramatic impacts on our life and our ability to be the best versions of ourselves. How you do the small things affects how you do the big things!

Delve into the habits that make up your routine. Ask better questions of yourself and really try to pinpoint whether your habits are resourceful or unresourceful. When making choices, listen to your gut feeling and ask yourself: "Does this move me closer to my goals?" If the answer is no, it's time to develop better habits.

MORNING PEOPLE KICK ASS

Would you get more done if you developed the habit of waking up at 5:00 a.m. to exercise and then began goal setting, vision mapping, and prioritizing the most important action steps of the day? All while the world is still asleep? (Remember, at these hours there are no distractions.)

Studies show a structured morning routine can make you more proactive—and happier.[4] What if you focused specifically on your goals and desires every morning by repeating them to yourself as a way of staying motivated and clear on who you need to be and what you need to do to achieve greatness? This could be a strong emotional reminder that will keep you laser focused for the day.

I personally have this as part of my morning success ritual. I always choose to start the day with the right motivation and inspiration to set myself up for success. This gives me an edge and massive advantage, particularly when there are challenges to face and bumps in the road. I will always work hard, sacrifice more, think bigger and face fears because I've done the work to shift my focus to the incredible outcome I'm working toward. I'm clear on who I need to be every single day, and through doing this I have engrained the wisdom that my WHY will always overcome the how. That's the truth that keeps me driving forward.

What is the ideal morning ritual to keep you on task and emotionally ready for the day and to not give into adversity?

DEVELOPING GOOD HABITS

According to a 2009 study from researchers from University College London, the average time it takes to form a new habit is 66 days (individual times varied from 18 to 254 days).[5] When a habit is cultivated, it becomes an automatic behavior, and willpower and effort are no longer required in order for you to complete and pursue your activity or ritual. When you get to this point, your habits and routines are then done on autopilot, which is why it's important to develop good habits.

When choosing habits, try to think critically about them and identify which ones will have a ripple effect and improve other areas of your life in positive ways, resulting in new and more resourceful habits. These are called keystone habits. Meditation is an example of a keystone habit because meditating regularly can decrease anxiety, promote better sleep, and increase your focus—all of which results in greater productivity!

If you want to try to develop a meditation habit, for example, you have to make it a permanent and easy-to-apply part of every day. You might:

- Set up a reminder for this new habit by scheduling a daily alarm/reminder on your phone.
- Write on your to-do list, "Fifteen minutes meditation, nonnegotiable!"
- Post a little sticker or photo of a Buddha on your mirror or wall.
- Join a meditation group! As we discussed in Chapter 8, having accountability partners can help us stay on track.
- Do a little research on meditation. Study the success of the people who inspire you, and model and reverse engineer the things they have done to achieve what they

have. Find out what their habits and rituals are—how often they train, what time of day, etc.

- Resourcefully reward yourself every time you meditate. This one will change your life, I promise! Most people have been conditioned to reward themselves with things that are unresourceful and don't help them to become awesome. They may celebrate completing a business project with unhealthy foods, or by getting drunk and taking party drugs, or by going on a random credit card shopping spree that they cannot afford. (If you're reading this, nodding to yourself, and thinking, *Yep, that's me*, you are not alone, and in all honesty, it's not your fault—this is how we have been taught to behave in movies and books and from our friends and family.) Instead, we need to reward ourselves resourcefully— healthy snacks, time with friends without the booze—to keep us motivated to continue the ritual until it sticks. List five resourceful rewards that will make you feel awesome and also have the effect of being good for you, things that you can implement now! Once you have a grand list of resourceful rewards, set little milestones for yourself, and once you achieve these milestones, you then treat yourself to something on that list and celebrate your wins!

HABIT CREATION MAP

Okay, I want to share with you an epic tool I use with my clients. It's called the Habit Creation Map. It's designed to help you create powerful habits, one at a time, and to have the clarity to ingrain them into your life with ease.

1. RESULTS *HAVE*

2. TIME OF DAY *WHEN*

3. ENVIRONMENT *WHERE*

4. FREQUENCY PER WEEK

5. ACTION STEPS *HOW*

- **Results: Have.** Establish the goal in mind that will be the result of your new ritual, and check in on your progress toward your eventual goal frequently in order to ensure that you are getting closer to it, or optimize the ritual to produce better results.
- **Time of the Day: When.** Be exact with the time you choose to do this, which will help you become the person who makes goals and commitments and then sticks to them. This is what people consider to be character! Don't beat yourself up if you miss a few days, but be committed to getting back on track.
- **Frequency Per Week.** Decide how many times per week you will do the ritual, and make it a nonnegotiable.
- **Environment: Where.** Use the same location for the ritual, preferably somewhere accessible where you can be every day. For instance, it could be meditating on your favorite chair.
- **Action Steps: How.** List out the exact recipe and routine for the way you structure your ritual. Remember that consistency is key, and if you want a habit to stick, then you must commit to sixty-six days of repeating the habit. Before you know it, this habit will become second nature.

Write down these categories or print out this sheet, and keep it somewhere within reach, so you see it daily—a kitchen bench or bedside table are good choices—in order to establish where you will attempt this habit. For each habit you wish to cultivate, use a new spreadsheet. Here's an example of a completed Habit Creation Map:

•   •   •

1. RESULTS *HAVE*

Step 1: Write down what you really want to have. This should be a result you want that will bring you satisfaction and fulfilment.

I want to have energy and focus on what's important for the day.

2. TIME OF DAY *WHEN*

Step 2: Write down the specific time of the day you will perform this habit.

In the mornings, first thing when I wake up from my alarm.

3. ENVIRONMENT *WHERE*

Step 3: Write down the specific place and any specific conditions you'll perform this habit in.

In bed, sitting up.

4. FREQUENCY PER WEEK

Step 4: Write down how often you will perform this habit.

Every day.

5. ACTION STEPS *HOW*

Step 5: Write down the simple action steps that you need to take to perform the habit completely.

1. Wake up without pressing the snooze button.

2. Kiss my partner good morning.

3. Sit up and drink a glass of water (already prepared the night before).

4. Think of ONE thing I'm grateful for.

5. Focus on Vision board and what each image means to me.

6. Take 4 Power breaths (Power breathing technique).

7. Take 3 deep breaths.

8. Recite my Values and what each means.

9. Take 3 deep breaths.

10. Recite my Mission and Goals to get me focused on what I need to do for the day.

11. Take 3 deep breaths.

Habits for Happiness

Looking for ideas for your Habit Creation Maps? There are certain keystone habits that we should be engaging in every day to become happier and healthy people. Here are just a few:

- **Make it a habit to get sunlight every day.** This boosts the body's Vitamin D supply and keeps our bones healthy and strong.
- **Make it a habit to engage in activities that create flow** (as discussed in Chapter 2).
- **Make it a habit to stop worrying.** Most of our worries in the Western world are irrational and unneeded anyway. Next time you have a thought about the future that causes anxiety, replace it with a positive thought: "What if I get everything I want in life?" Train yourself to nip negative thoughts in the bud before you end up in negative thought loops and a downward spiral.
- **Make it a habit to eat right.** The proper fuel boosts energy and creative thought.
- **Make it a habit to get a good night's sleep.** Virtually every successful person touts the benefits of quality sleep! Improving your sleep quality will result in a myriad of benefits. It will increase productivity, happiness, and focus, and decrease stress.

TIPS FOR A GOOD NIGHT'S SLEEP

- Sleeping at consistent hours—and when it is dark—will make you happier, healthier, and more focused.
- Eight hours of constant sleep is a good amount; although as you get older, you generally need less.

- Use your bedroom for sleeping, and only for sleeping (don't watch TV or do work there). If you do this, you will train your brain to feel tired when you are in your bedroom, almost like a Pavlovian response to entering your room.
- Establish a bedroom ritual. Your mind needs to relax. A bedtime ritual could include brushing your teeth, drinking some herbal tea, light reading, or meditation, anything that relaxes you.
- Avoid caffeine near bedtime. Personally, I avoid it after 1:00 p.m. daily. Even if you can fall asleep after having coffee, it still disrupts you from having quality deep sleep.
- Don't eat a large meal within three hours before sleeping or else it leaves you susceptible to indigestion or acid reflux, lowering the quality of your sleep.
- Drink some water before sleep but not too much or you will wake up in the night needing to use the toilet!
- Add some background or white noise if you have difficulty sleeping in silence. After all, for thousands of years of evolution, humans had been used to sleeping with the noises of nature! Nature sounds or rain tracks can help you manage the silence and achieve deeper sleep.

"Comfort is the killer of creativity." —DAVID CHOE

- **Make it a habit to be uncomfortable.** We've talked a lot about leaving your comfort zone in this book on your way to becoming a leader. You need to make it a habit. If you are an artist, you should be pushing your limits all the time and going beyond what you have previously done in order to innovate and push your boundaries of creativity and language. Learn to step on your tail and be okay with it. If you're shy, make conversation with strangers, which will open up all sorts of pathways in life that you never knew existed. Start by saying "hi" while you are in an elevator or waiting in line—a lot of people have a story they are willing to share.

- **Make it a habit to be a lifelong learner.** Invest in yourself by investing in books and seminars and by finding mentors. People who know me know that I am a reading machine! I absolutely love books and audiobooks and have been reading an average of one to two books per week for the last five years! Don't view a book written by a successful person and see it for its price; see it as what its return could be. Where is that million-dollar paragraph?! Sometimes I'll be sitting in my office reading an incredible biography from a person who has changed the world in some way, and I get this sudden overwhelming sensation of gratitude that I have the opportunity and privilege to learn from this person's life experiences, challenges, and triumphs without ever personally knowing them—for the ridiculous price of $20 and my time! See how lucky we are!

BREAKING BAD HABITS

Bad habits. We all have them. Waiting until the absolute last minute to begin a project. Stopping at a fast-food drive thru for dinner because we're too lazy to cook. If we aren't preparing for our goals, we will get distracted and lose track of what we want, and we will start to give into temptations of instant gratification and unresourceful choices. These things act as sedation tools, distractions to keep us from facing the "uncomfortable" steps into greatness.

Breaking bad habits can be tricky business, but here are some tips to get your started:

1. **Become aware of bad habits.** Awareness is the first step to conquering! Now that you know how much sugar you're taking in, you can do something about it!
2. **Replace bad habits with healthier habits.** Reach for the banana instead of the Danish at your next morning meeting.
3. **Instead of saying "I can't," try saying, "I don't."** You'd be surprised what kind of impact that will have on you!
4. **Visualize!** See yourself stomping on that cigarette or tossing the cheeseburger into the trash. How do you feel? Then try doing it for real!
5. **Start with one bad habit.** When you try to change too many habits at once, you can become overwhelmed.

The good thing about habits is that they are not permanent. With the right focus and attention, we are able to have control over the habits that shape our lives. If you miss a day or two, don't beat yourself up. Just refocus, and start again. There are always going to be slight setbacks and times where we sleep in or just give in to the easier choice. But as long as we are committed to moving forward and are making a conscious effort to change and grow every day, in the long run the little setbacks and slipups are less important. Make it a habit for life to keep getting up when you get knocked down. That's how you win!

We are what we do, even when we're not paying attention. Get good at making sure your habits don't cause you to stray from your path. But when they do—and they will!—gently guide yourself back on track, and you'll become an even stronger and more in control leader than you were before.

SUMMING UP

- There are two types of habits. Resourceful habits move us closer to our goals. Unresourceful habits place roadblocks on our path to success.

- Habits, even the smallest ones, affect us in big ways. That one piece of candy or drink you have each day may seem like a tiny deal, but it can have a cumulative effort on your health and your output!

- Identify your keystone habits. These have a ripple effect and improve your life in positive ways!

- Find ways to make these habits a part of your life. Use reminders, photos, research, accountability partners, resourceful rewards—whatever it takes!

- Create a Habit Creation Map. This will serve as a reminder of the new habit you seek, as well as the time of day, frequency, environment, and action steps needed to make it stick.

CHAPTER 10

CREATING YOUR SUCCESS ENVIRONMENT

"It is better to light a candle than curse the darkness."
—WILLIAM L. WATKINSON

Society is always changing. Now, more than ever, how we live, how we work, and how we communicate is being shaped by technology. How many times have you gone out with friends and found that all of you were standing around silently on your phones? Millions of people have social media accounts and visit them daily. A recent Gallup poll showed that 43 percent of employed Americans spend at least part of their time working from home,[1] which means they are working alone, communicating to the office via computer.

At the same time, we also live in an insecure society, arguably exacerbated by technology. People feel the urge—from the safety of their homes and offices and wherever they are—to comment on everything we do, from what we wear, to where we go, to how we raise our kids, which has the power to put filters on what we feel comfortable saying. Many times, if you talk about your success, you will be considered an egomaniac or appear to be gloating. If you talk about how much money you make, it's considered rude. And yet if you talk about how poor you are and how much you are struggling, that is acceptable and will elicit sympathy from your peers. Why is this? In part, it's because people often feel "attacked" when they see others around them achieving and succeeding. They feel like they are less when other people are more, and they want to find the faults in others' success so they can rationalize why they, themselves, have not experienced that same result. It's what we call in Australia "tall poppy syndrome," a classic scarcity-driven mindset that is based on jealousy that seems to have spread globally like a virus. Tall poppy syndrome stops people from becoming the best version of themselves because they're so busy tearing down, attacking, criticizing, and resenting others that they're not focusing on their own path.

The truth is that there is not some finite amount of success to go around. There is abundance, more than enough for everyone, and we can all live successful lives. The good news is if you have ever suffered from tall poppy syndrome, you can change. As we've learned, with practice and time, we can reprogram our minds, open ourselves up, and learn to be better—in this case, we can learn to be truly happy for others' successes. Most importantly, we can start learning from THEM—asking better questions about their thinking and their level of action and energy. (Success always leaves clues!)

SHOW ME YOUR FRIENDS, AND I WILL SHOW YOU YOUR FUTURE!

Of course, the problem of tall poppy syndrome doesn't always have to do with us and how we feel about others' success. Many times, it has to do with others and how THEY view YOUR success.

You might say, "Well, who cares?" As we've discussed in this book, your eyes should be on your own path, and that's true. But no leader is an island. We may have this illusion that our thoughts, behaviors, and decisions are entirely ours and that the people and things around us don't dictate and influence us, but the truth is that most of what we are—and do—is a result of the exterior world and our influences. And we need to be aware of that.

As children, our worldview is manufactured by our parents' beliefs in a big way. Think about the food you eat, the place you live, the way you dress, your spiritual beliefs—chances are, they came from your parents. You probably didn't actively try to imitate them, but all these things seep in, like osmosis, and become a part of us, whether we like it or not. That's not to say we should let ourselves be a victim of our past! As you know, we can always change, but we need to accept that the people around us, then and now, and the information they present is going to be a contributor to our happiness and success. Never underestimate how much our friends, family, and colleagues shape our worldview!

That's why we need to be careful about the people we choose to surround ourselves with (see chart). We need to ask ourselves: Do I feel inspired after being with this person? Or do I feel agitated and depressed? And then we need to follow our gut—often your gut knows better than the conscious mind! We are connected, and the positive behaviors and habits will rub off on us. We mirror and learn from the people in our environment, so defend yours, protect your mental and emotional space, and surround yourself with a community that will help you rise!

. . .

WHO TO KEEP? WHO TO CUT?

KEEP COLUMN	CUT COLUMN
Positive thinkers and talkers	Negative thinkers and talkers
People who think big	People who gossip or bitch and moan
People who push you out of your comfort zone	People who hold you back
People who make you feel hopeful	People who make you feel depressed
People who are smart or desire to be smarter	People who have no desire to learn
People who are achieving success	People who laugh at others' success
People who are striving to improve themselves	People who criticize others' efforts
People with high aspirations	People who have low/no aspirations
People who are motivated	People who are complacent
People you want to emulate	People you "feel sorry for"
People with open minds	People with closed minds
People with big, open hearts	People with Grinch-sized hearts

ASSEMBLE TEAM AWESOME

Motivational speaker Jim Rohn famously said that we are the average of the five people we hang around with the most. (In our technologically driven age, this might be the five people we interact with the most online!) In my own life, I find that when I chose to be around mentors and people who are smarter than I am or have achieved more than I have, I became more focused, which improved both my business and relationships. Now it's time to create the success environment that YOU deserve.

Step 1: Assess Your Current Team

1. List the five people who you converse and spend the most time with. (If you're a parent or guardian, don't include children.)
2. Next to their name, list the main activity you do with them or the type of relationship you have.
3. Check whether or not they encourage you or discourage you.
4. Reflect on the results you've been getting in your life with these people around you:
5. Are you spending time kicking goals, or are you binging TV shows?
6. Are you taking action, or are you still just talking about your dreams?
7. Are your conversations inspiring, or are they focused on the negatives?
8. Circle any names in your list whom you've checked as someone who encourages you and you feel adds positively to your progress.

CURRENT TEAM		
NAME	ACTIVITY/ RELATIONSHIP	ENCOURAGE/ DISCOURAGE
1.		
2.		
3.		

CURRENT TEAM (CONT.)		
NAME	ACTIVITY/ RELATIONSHIP	ENCOURAGE/ DISCOURAGE
4.		
5.		

Step 2: Assemble Your New Team

1. From the list above, write down those who encourage you and whom you want to keep spending time with. (Whether you have one, two, three, four, five, or none, be honest and focused on your results when assessing who makes the cut in your new team.)
2. To fill your team, think of people in your life that:
   - Inspire you
   - Keep you accountable
   - Tell you the truth (not just what you want to hear)
   - Are smarter than you
   - Have the same or similar results in the field or industry you're looking to succeed in
3. Write down the attributes of this person (e.g., persistent, tenacious, disciplined, focused, calm), the special power or ability they have (e.g., influence, empathy, compassion, knowledge) especially when times are tough and things seem impossible.

NEW AWESOME TEAM	
NAME	**ATTRIBUTES**
1.	
2.	
3.	
4.	
5.	

Step 3: Ascend with Your New Team

1. Spend more time with these five people:
   - Go out for coffee
   - Go out for a walk
   - Chat on the phone
   - Chat online
   - Sit down for a meal
2. Grow and cultivate your relationship with these five people by:
   - Asking them questions and taking action on the advice they give.
   - Reporting back how their advice worked (or not) and what you did to make it work.
   - Adding value to their lives in any way you can.
   - Always being thankful and showing your appreciation.

Conduct this exercise periodically to ensure you are surrounding yourself with those with the best of intentions and who will help you put your best foot forward and create the best version of you.

HANDLING NAYSAYERS

There's one in virtually every bunch. (Hopefully, only one.) The people who tell you that you can't, you won't, you shouldn't, you'll never. Unfortunately, sometimes these naysayers are people that you love—and, deep down, love you—and mean well but get hit with a level of fear based on your growth and need for change. You stepping up and shining like never before often initially scares the people around us because it forces them to ask themselves questions that potentially shine a light on things they don't like about themselves. Their insecurities about being good enough, or you outgrowing them, start to arise.

As weird as this sounds, I love to view the moments when a naysayer tells me what I can and can't do as a test from the universe. I see it as a challenge to see if I'm really worthy of this amazing change and goals/outcome I want. I say to myself, "If I really deserve this, would I let someone else's tainted opinion stop me from becoming the person I know I'm destined to be?" So I push on, and in the face of the naysayers, doubters, and negativity, I continue to step up!

Here are a couple other important things to remember when dealing with naysayers and cynical people:

- **Just because someone close to you tells that something is awful, evil, or bad for you, doesn't mean you have to agree!** Technology, and social media, in particular, seems to encourage a "herd mentality," which means people can be influenced by their peers to adopt certain ways of thinking for no rational reason. We've all seen the commenters who like to jump on the bandwagon because they think agreeing with everyone else makes them smart—or right. It doesn't.

- **Just because other people believe that your ideas are hopeless or crazy doesn't mean they are!** As we discussed in Chapter 4, a lot of people live in fear—they fear change, looking silly, failing, and so much more. These people will set mediocre goals and only want to live mediocre lives because the thought of anything else makes them extremely uncomfortable. They have given up on having big dreams a long time ago. So if you talk about your big dreams or your plan to build a business or transform your body, they will most likely tell you it can't be done or you will fail. Don't take it personally. It is them projecting their own insecurities and inadequacies into the conversation and onto you.

The awesome part about this, and a great lesson for all you growing leaders out there, is that when you lead by example, when you continue to fight for what you believe in and live your TRUTH, even the naysayers will start to look up to you and see how amazing what you are doing really is. They often turn from naysayer into "interested inquirer," and then hopefully one day they can step into their own greatness, all because you were brave enough to shine when everyone else was to afraid to!

* * *

THE NAYSAYER CHECKLIST

This is a simple guide to see if a person is acting like a naysayer and how to manage them. When someone in your life offers their opinion or tells you that what you're attempting to do can't be done, follow these simple steps:

Step 1: Qualify

Ask yourself: Is this person considered an expert in the field or industry that you're aiming to succeed in?

If yes, then ask yourself:

- Are they considered successful in the field or industry?
- Are their successes valued by the field or industry?
- Have they been operating in the field or industry for longer than five years?

If the answer to all of these questions is still yes, then it might be worth considering their opinion.

If the answer is no at any point, move on to Step 2.

Step 2: Be Grateful

Presuppose that this person means well. Always come from a place of love and gratitude. Simply reply with gratitude and offer no room for further discussion. You can say:

- "Thanks, I appreciate you looking out for me."
- "That's awesome that we can have different opinions. Thanks for sharing yours."
- "Thank you."

Keep it simple and short, and say it with a tone that shows you're grateful for them meaning well.

Step 3: Reaffirm

Make sure you reconnect with your purpose, mission, and values if you feel doubt and you're second-guessing yourself. Reaffirm what completing your goals and succeeding means to you and your loved ones. Turn up the volume to the sounds of success, and the naysayers' voices will fade away.

You may be a product of your upbringing but creating a successful environment NOW is all in your hands. You have the power to NOT READ social media comments. You have the power to SPEAK UP when well-meaning people cross the line. You have the power to ELIMINATE naysayers from your Team Awesome. You have the power to BELIEVE in your goals and dreams, even if no one else does. If you have a goal that people say is impossible, but there is goodness in it, it is noble, and will help the world on a large scale, you MUST go for it. Remember, so many of the things that make up the world today would have been inconceivable to the vast majority of people one hundred or two hundred years ago. (Years ago, people actually wrote books about why it was impossible for planes to exist!) If you can believe it, you can achieve it, and I want you to know that I personally have your back.

No leader is an island. Leaders are tall skyscrapers within a landscape of many buildings.

●   ●   ●

SUMMING UP

- The people you surround yourself with have the power to influence you. But you have the power to recognize that and do something about it. Once we acknowledge the chatter, we can choose what voices to listen to.
- Some people feel the need to bring you down to pull themselves up. In Australia, this is known as "tall poppy syndrome" and stems from jealousy, plain and simple.
- To assemble your Team Awesome, assess the people you spend the most time with, assemble a new team that includes those who encourage you, and cultivate relationships with your new team.
- Manage naysayers. Tune out the criticisms, and turn up the success!

CHAPTER 11

THE ACTION PLAN

"Fear and Resistance cannot live in action."
—ANDY ANDERSON

We are coming to the end of my first book! By now, I hope you are inspired and determined to craft your values and vision in life, set goals to achieve it, change your thinking to a "relentlessly optimistic" mindset, build good habits and motivation, and block out the haters and the self-doubt. Now it's time to take action on the road to becoming a true leader!

ACTION PLAN TEMPLATE

An Action Plan can help motivate you to take the steps you need to become the Ultimate You and can be written up with these simple sections in mind:

• • •

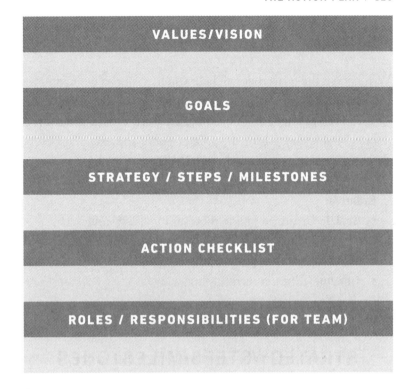

VALUES/VISION

GOALS

STRATEGY / STEPS / MILESTONES

ACTION CHECKLIST

ROLES / RESPONSIBILITIES (FOR TEAM)

VALUES/VISION

If you haven't already, write down your values and vision. Make sure you've written your Life Purpose Statement. You will reference these in everything you do.

Example:
- **My Values:** Love, Health, and Legacy
- **My Vision:** A world where my family can live healthy, happy, loving, and fulfilled lives.
- **My Life Purpose Statement:** To create a community of healthy, happy people doing incredible things.

GOALS

Write down the goals that will help you live your values and move you closer to your vision. Remember to make your goals CHANGE: challenging, heartfelt, actionable with a deadline, nonnegotiable, geared for the greater good, and exact. For every goal, you'll create a separate Action Plan.

Example:
- **Goal 1:** Create an online community of like-minded people that can contribute to an ongoing conversation about health and fulfillment.
- **Timeline:** Three months.

STRATEGY/STEPS/MILESTONES

Write down an overall strategy that's going to help you accomplish your goal. This is where it's necessary to get guidance from mentors and people who've succeeded in the area you want to succeed in. Make sure the strategy can be broken down into steps that you can follow and tangible milestones that you can measure.

Example:
- **My Strategy for Goal 1:** Create an online community on Facebook to utilize its functions.
- **Steps for my Strategy:**
  - **Step 1:** Create a Facebook Group and invite an initial group of 100 people (family and friends).
  - **Step 2:** Launch Facebook Group to the public, and invite friends and family to share the group.

- **Step 3:** Continue to add value and content to the group until group members begin to create their own content and the number of members reach 500.
- **My Milestones:**
  - Soft launch for family and friends.
  - Launch for public.
  - Total members, 100.
  - Total members, 500.

ACTION CHECKLIST

To accelerate your success, all your actions must be purposeful and focused on driving results. Use this checklist for all the actions you write down on your Action Checklist.

- ☐ Will this action see you closer to your vision?
- ☐ Will this action help to complete your goal?
- ☐ Will this action help you feel congruent with the person who you want to become?
- ☐ Is this action part of the current strategy? If not, will this action fit into the strategy?
- ☐ Is this action accomplishing a milestone?
- ☐ Can this action be completed within the day? If not, can this action be broken into smaller actions?
- ☐ Do you know exactly how to perform this action? If not, does there need to be research or study done as an additional action?
- ☐ Can a deadline be set for this action?

If the answer is yes to all of these items on the checklist, then the action should be taken.

Examples:

- **Action:** Research five similar successful groups and pages on Facebook to see what's in trend.
- **Action:** Create ten posts that offer value in preparation for launch.
- **Action:** Design Facebook profile image and banner image.

ROLES/RESPONSIBILITIES

If you're working with a team, consider how you and your team can collaborate and cooperate. Is there anyone else (on your team) who can perform this action instead of you? If so, can this action be delegated?

Example: Design of Facebook profile and banner image can be outsourced.

Keeping track of your progress is imperative to your journey. Write out each action—in detail—that you will take weekly to achieve your goals. When you've taken an action, cross it out on the Action Plan. This will make you feel satisfied, accomplished, and heroic! Your brain will sense that you are accomplishing something, and you will itch to move forward, excited at the new person you are becoming!

> *"Twenty years from now you will be more disappointed by the things that you didn't do than by the ones you did do. So throw off the bowlines. Sail away from the safe harbor. Catch the trade winds in your sails. Explore. Dream. Discover."*
> **—MARK TWAIN**

To achieve massive success, you can plan, set goals, and dream all you want, but no thoughts, plans, dreams, or aspirations will come to be without taking action. Make your mantra, "I am a person of action!" Act as if you only had months to live and no time to waste. Start your journey now, not tomorrow or next week! Seize the moment. Don't let opportunities slip through your fingers. Decide when and where you will begin to work and be as specific as possible. Then do it!

Congratulations! You are now a warrior on the road to leadership and success. This is where our journey together ends for now. As you march down your path, you will come to stop signs, forks in the road, and rocks in your way. View all as a challenge, an opportunity, and a learning experience, and be sure to revisit your goals, Habit Maps, and Motivational Matrices regularly. This is the mindset of the warrior and of someone destined for greatness! I made it, and you can as well. Be healthy, be well, be all you can be, and do whatever it takes to Unleash the Ultimate You.

SUMMING UP

- An effective Action Plan consists of five sections: values/ vision, goals, strategies/steps/milestones, action checklist, and roles/responsibilities (if you are working in a team).
- Make sure to write out each action in detail on a weekly basis, crossing it out in your Action Plan when it has been completed.
- Use the Action Checklist to ensure that all planned actions are appropriate and should be taken.

NOTES

INTRODUCTION

1. Steven Pressfield, *The War of Art: Break Through the Blocks and Win Your Inner Creative Battles* (New York: Warner Books, 2003), 12.

CHAPTER 4

1. Sandra Blakeslee, "Beliefs Reported to Shorten Life," *New York Times*, November 7, 1993.

CHAPTER 5

1. LD Kublansky and RC Thurston, "Emotional vitality and incident coronary heart disease: benefits of healthy psychological functioning," *Arch Gen Psychiatry* 64, no. 12 (December 2007): 1393–401, https://www.ncbi.nlm.nih.gov/pubmed/18056547.

2. Martin E.P. Seligman, *Learned Optimism: How to Change Your Mind and Your Life* (New York: Knopf Doubleday, 2011), 4–5.

CHAPTER 6

1. Sonja Lyubomirsky, Laura King, and Ed Diener, "The benefits of frequent positive affect: Does happiness lead to success?" *Psychological Bulletin* 131, no. 6 (2005): 803–855.

2. Sonja Lyubomirsky, Kennon M. Sheldon, and David Schkade, "Pursuing happiness: The architecture of sus-

tainable change," *Review of General Psychology* 9, no.2 (June 2005): 111–131.

3. Erin M. Shackell and Lionel G. Standing, "Mind Over Matter: Mental Training Increases Physical Strength," *North American Journal of Psychology* 9, no. 1 (March 2007).

4. AJ Adams, "Seeing Is Believing: The Power of Visualization," *Psychology Today* (December 3, 2009), https://www.psychologytoday.com/us/blog/flourish/200912/seeing-is-believing-the-power-visualization.

5. Todd Gilchrist, "Interview: Will Smith," *IGN* (December 8, 2016), https://www.ign.com/articles/2006/12/18/interview-will-smith?page=2.

6. Alice Winkler, "What It Takes: Oprah Winfrey, Part 1," *VOA Learning English* (September 1, 2017), https://learningenglish.voanews.com/a/what-it-takes-oprah-winfrey-1/3993224.html.

CHAPTER 7

1. Tony Robbins, "Gratitude Is the Solution to Anger and Fear," *Thrive Global* (November 29, 2016), https://medium.com/thrive-global/tony-robbins-gratitude-is-the-solution-to-anger-and-fear-c3fa819825c.

2. Iqtidar Ali, "How Elon Musk Saved SpaceX and Tesla at the Same Time," *EVANNEX* (July 8, 2018), https://evannex.com/blogs/news/how-elon-musk-saved-spacex-and-tesla-at-the-same-time.

3. Kate Taylor, "How Howard Schultz went from living in Brooklyn public housing to growing Starbucks into an $84 billion business," *Business Insider* (December 13, 2017), https://www.businessinsider.com/starbucks-howard-schultz-success-story-2017-12.

4. Charles Clark and Madeline Stone, "The incredible and inspiring life story of Alibaba founder Jack Ma, one of the richest people in China," *Business Insider* (March 2, 2017),

https://www.businessinsider.com/inspiring-life-story
-of-alibaba-founder-jack-ma-2017-2.
5. Davide "Foletto" Casali, "'Focusing is about saying no'—
Steve Jobs," *YouTube* (June 26, 2011), https://www.youtube
.com/watch?v=H8eP99neOVs.

CHAPTER 8

1. Naser Hoboubi, Alireza Choobineh, Fatemeh Kamari
Ghanavati, Sareh Keshavarzi, and Ali Akbar Hosseini, "The
Impact of Job Stress and Job Satisfaction on Workforce
Productivity in an Iranian Petrochemical Industry," *Safety
and Health at Work* 8, no.1 (March 2017): 67–71, https://
www.ncbi.nlm.nih.gov/pmc/articles/PMC5355527/.
2. Stephen Newland, "The Power of Accountability," *Association for Financial Counseling & Planning Education*
(2018), https://www.afcpe.org/news-and-publications/the
-standard/2018-3/the-power-of-accountability/.

CHAPTER 9

1. Nicole M. Avena, Pedro Rada, and Bartley G. Hoebel,
"Evidence for sugar addiction: Behavioral and neuro-
chemical effects of intermittent, excessive sugar intake,"
Neuroscience & Biobehavioal Reviews 32, no. 1 (2008):
20–39, https://www.ncbi.nlm.nih.gov/pmc/articles/PMC
2235907/.
2. "Added Sugars," *American Heart Association* (April 17,
2018), https://www.heart.org/en/healthy-living/healthy
-eating/eat-smart/sugar/added-sugars.
3. Alice G. Walton, "How Much Sugar Are Americans
Eating?" *Forbes* (August 30, 2012), https://www.forbes.
com/sites/alicegwalton/2012/08/30/how-much-sugar
-are-americans-eating-infographic/#60a014934ee7.
4. Samuel E. Jones, Jacqueline M. Lane, Michael N. Wee-
don, et. al, "Genome-wide association analyses of chrono-

type in 697,828 individuals provides insights into circadian rhythms," *Nature Communications* 10, no. 33 (2019), https://www.nature.com/articles/s41467-018-08259-7.

5. Phillippa Lally, Cornelia H. M. Van Jaarsveld, Henry W. W. Potts, and Jane Wardle, "How are habits formed: Modelling habit formation in the real world," *European Journal of Social Psychology* 40, (2010): 998–1009, http://repositorio.ispa.pt/bitstream/10400.12/3364/1/IJSP_998-1009.pdf.

CHAPTER 10

1. Annamarie Mann and Amy Adkins, "America's Coming Workplace: Home Alone," *Business Journal* (March 15, 2017), https://news.gallup.com/businessjournal/206033/america-coming-workplace-home-alone.aspx.

FURTHER READING

Bet-David, Patrick. *Doing the Impossible: The 25 Laws for Doing the Impossible*. United States: Valuetainment Publishing, 2012.

Broad, Eli. *The Art of Being Unreasonable: Lessons in Unconventional Thinking*. Hoboken, NJ: John Wiley & Sons, 2012.

Covey, Stephen. *The 7 Habits of Highly Effective People*. New York: Simon & Schuster, 2013.

Dweck, Carol. *Mindset: The New Psychology of Success*. New York: Random House, 2006.

Ecko, Marc. *Unlabel: Selling You Without Selling Out*. New York: Touchstone, 2015.

Gladwell, Malcolm. *Outliers: The Story of Success*. New York: Little Brown & Company, 2008.

Isaacson, Walter. *Steve Jobs*. New York: Simon & Schuster, 2011.

Pearson, Sharon. *Ultimate You: Heal. Reclaim. Become. Live Your Awesome Life*. Sydney: Waterside Publishing, 2019.

Pickens, T. Boone. *The First Billion Is the Hardest: Reflections on a Life of Comebacks and America's Energy Future*. New York: Crown Business, 2008.

Seligman, Martin E. P., PhD. *Learned Optimism: How to Change Your Mind and Your Life*. New York: Vintage Books, 2006.

Schultz, Howard. *Pour Your Heart Into It: How Starbucks Built a Company One Cup at a Time.* New York: Hachette, 1997.

Tracy, Brian. *Eat That Frog! 21 Great Ways to Stop Procrastinating and Get More Done in Less Time.* Oakland, CA: Berrett-Koehler Publishers, 2017.

Vance, Ashlee. *Elon Musk: Tesla, SpaceX, and the Quest for a Fantastic Future.* New York: HarperCollins, 2015.